Dedicated to Prof. Adolfas Mekas & St. Tula

FILMMAKING

AGAINST

THE CURRENT

–

NOTES ABOUT MAKING

A FILM

"FOR THE BLINDS"

Written & Designed

by

Ozan D. Adam

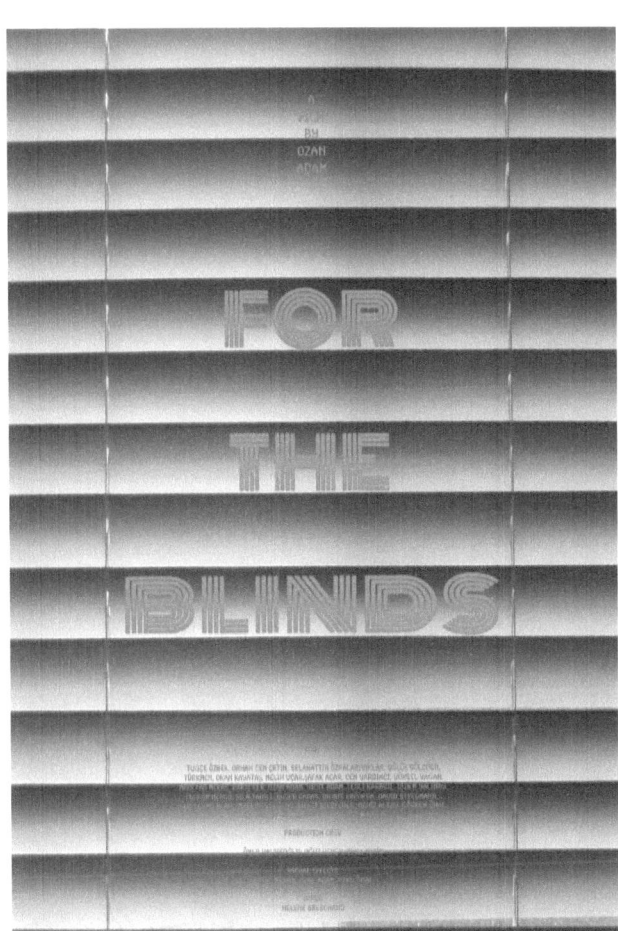

Ozan Adam studied art and cinema at Bard College, attended The New School University for his MA. He worked as an independent artist and as a professional in film production, advertising, commercials, media, stage construction and design industries in New York. His body of diverse artwork consists of text; design, illustration, painting, sculpture, animation, film, video and installations which have been exhibited in solo and collective exhibitions at many prestigious international exhibitions, biennials, museums, galleries and festivals around the world.

He wrote a novel titled "The Manifesto About A Man Who Threw A Stone Into The Sky And Followed It" and translated it into English with the supervision of Prof. William Weaver who is the translator of many of the books of Umberto Eco and Italo Calvino. Many of his books including his artworks and his novels were published and are available online. His film "Zymotic-Amaurosis" was awarded with the Special Jury Award in the 14th International Ankara Film Festival and another film of his titled "The Two Names of A Testimony About The Execution of A Happening and A Suitcase Full of Broken Records" was awarded as the Best Experimental Film in the 17th International Ankara Film Festival. He taught many courses and gave numerous lectures at many universities and has been invited by universities and institutions such as Middle Eastern Technical University, Bosphorus University, The Netherlands Institute of Higher Education, Aksanat Art Foundation and The Bauhaus Foundation in Germany for workshops, conferences and seminars. He has taught graduate and undergraduate level courses and supervised internationally awarded projects since 2001.

He directed commercials, advertisement campaigns and music videos. He has also served as a jury member for universities and the award juries of film festivals. Many of his artworks and films have been selected, awarded and presented by festivals, galleries and museums worldwide.

His films were screened at Martin Gropius-Bau Museum, Haus der Kulturen der Welt in Berlin, Louvre Museum and Pompidou Art Center in Paris, National Centre for Visual Arts, Reina Sofia National Museum in Madrid, Aksanat Gallery, Proje 4L Contemporary Art Museum, Platform Garanti Contemporary Art Center, Tate Modern in London, the 10th Venice Biennale in Venice and at The New Museum in New York and Tokyo. His works have been exhibited at many international solo and collective exhibitions some of which are RECONTRES INTERNATIONALES PARIS / BERLIN / MADRID, CENTRE POMPIDOU, JEU DE PAUMENATIONAL MUSEUM PARIS / REINA SOFIA NATIONAL MUSEUM, MADRID / HAUS DER KULTUREN DER WELT, BERLIN, ISTANBUL MODERN ART MUSEUM, 28th & 33rd ISTANBUL FILM FESTİVAL, SMALL CHANGES / OPENDOOR, Akbank Gallery, MISSING MOMENTS, Deform Art Gallery, OXIMOXI ART EXHIBITION, INTERNATIONAL ISTANBUL BIENNIAL, BACK TO THE CORE, Platform Garanti Contemporary Art Center / Tate Modern, LONDON, OPEN LIBRARY EXHIBITION, Platform Garanti Contemporary Art Center, 10th VENICE BIENNALE, VENICE, FOCUS ISTANBUL EXHIBITION, BERLIN, Berliner Pool Exhibition, MARTIN GROPIUS BAU MUSEUM, BERLIN, Bauhaus Foundation Group Exhibition, LUMENANCE OF THE MOON, USA, EUROPE &

ASIA, I AM TOO SAD TO KILL YOU!, PROJE 4L CONTEMPORARY ART MUSEUM, THE PERSISTENCE OF LOW END AMBIENT VISION, AKBANK CULTURE & ART CENTER, OVERKILL, HEERESBACKEREI-KULTUR, BERLIN,NEW MUSEUM, NEW YORK & TOKYO.

His feature film "For The Blinds" won the Special Jury Award at the Indian Cine Festival in Mumbai, received excellent reviews and it has been screened at Istanbul Modern Museum and Pera Museum in Istanbul. As the director of the first internationally awarded Turkish science fiction feature film that is not a comedy, an animation, a cult film or a remake he marks his place in the history of cinema.

Synopsis

The stories in the film take place in parallel realities where people live only for a very limited time as one character. The memories of the people are erased periodically and replaced with new ones. Adjustments are made on the details of the new memories so that everybody remembers himself or herself as if they have always been living as that character for their entire life.

The film also metaphorically addresses the destruction of the identity and memory of the masses. It is a reflection on the daily urban, social, technological, political and global transformations. The spaces, streets, cities and the entire culture are in such an extremely rapid state of flux and transformation that it is as if the past is being erased and since the memories of the society are being destroyed, the identity of the individuals are being deleted and therefore social identity is demolished and artificially reconstructed. The rate, the scale and the level of this social and global transformation cause the degeneration of the society and the commodification of the identity, which leads to a form of massive social schizophrenia.

Seintn's memories can not be entirely deleted therefore he suffers from multiple personality syndrome and he has no other way but to live with the bits and pieces of the memories of other people. He lives in oblivion to his condition. The detectives are after him for the "crimes" he has committed suspecting that he is a delirious serial killer who is responsible for numerous crimes and murders, yet the stories unravel differently than expected.

www.fortheblinds.com

Having arrived at the location where some of my ideas about the film were consolidated, I decided to write down some of my thoughts about the long and arduous process of making the film and to indite some of the matters which had aroused in my mind during the making of the film and afterwards. It is not merely because I think that the film is very important, but because of the fact that for many years before I made it, almost everybody told me that it was impossible to make, because I believe that telling the story of making such a rigorous film pretty much on my own without a budget or sponsors or any financial support, except of course for the voluntary help of some of my students, assistants, friends and my family, and sharing this unique challenging production process might help some people who are interested in cinema, people who want to make films and the new generations to come. And also one other reason behind it is because I might forget some of the details and some of my thoughts as time passes, if I do not write them down. I won't just write about the making of the film. I intend to write also about many subjects such as science, art, history, sociology and cinema. I taught film courses, gave workshops, seminars at universities and institutions and attended conferences as a speaker for about 15 years. I had the chance to share my views about cinema, art and related topics and my experience with the participants, audiences and my students over the years. For the sake of passing on some of my experiences I can only hope that by sharing some of my thoughts, knowledge and the adventure of making this no budget film which was said to be impossible to make without professional actors, actresses and many things that are said to be a must; it might cast a light on a new perspective for film students and for many people who want to make films. For all the years I was teaching film courses I thought that cinema is very much like poetry and therefore I thought that one could not teach someone how to make films just as one can not teach how to write poetry yet what I can do is to share my views based on my own experiences, the films I watched, the books I have read and my own thoughts and hope to inspire and that is what I aspire to do with this book.

My dear professor Prof. Adolfas Mekas used to advise us to write poetry instead of making films. He used to give that advice because films are very expensive to make yet you just need a piece of paper and a pencil to write poetry. He was right in a way, people do not read poetry much, therefore poetry reaches out to less people compared to cinema yet that does not mean that it has a narrower or more limited potential for expression. Actually, on the contrary, it's has an extraordinary capacity. Since poetry uses words rather than images it allows the imagination to foster more and motivates the mind to think more abstractly. Poetry is similar to experimental cinema where as narrative film is the equivalent of prose. The narrative structure that is composed of simple elements such as the beginning, development and conclusion is most commonly used in blockbuster movies as in most novels and stories. Since they use a simpler, linear narrative sometimes with flashbacks and flash forwards, they're easier to engage with and follow and they have been vastly promoted and marketed all around the world therefore they are more common than poetic, abstract and experimental films. Just as in poetry, experimental cinema also liberates the mind because its essence is to develop its own original and genuine abstract form of expression without imposing a simple, realistic, linear narrative. In that sense it allows the spectator to establish relations between the images and interpret them freely just as it happens in the dream state.

Sometimes one can think that writing is unnecessary because one assumes that everyone can think the same things that one does. Yet you might be the first one to think about it in that way. They say that great minds think alike but sometimes the person who might not even have a great mind can come up with a very minute and simple idea that can change the world. Or at least other people can be inspired by that idea or observation which may allow them to come up with grand thoughts. For example Einstein might have been inspired by some of the ideas behind the inventions and theories that he encountered while he was working at the patent office and they might have helped him to think differently about the possibilities. Ideas, however, might seem to be absurd or unnecessary or impossible. Some of them, over time, can become important or inspire others, transform and change societies, individuals, philosophies, sciences, beliefs, assumptions and prejudices. Therefore sharing some meaningless and superfluous thoughts or at least making notes about them can be beneficial and that is why I am trying to write down some of my ideas, experiences, views and also some of the questions that are stuck in the labyrinths of my mind.

When there are limited number of papers to write on or if the time is limited because of the fact that there might be a power outage or for some other reason, one should be considered to be in a position where one has to be very careful about the way one chooses the words to express oneself, yet when there is a limitation on the number of pages to write on one calculates one's words very precisely to express oneself in as fewer words as possible to be able to fit one's thoughts into the little space on the page as much as possible but when there is limited time one does not have a choice. This makes me realize that the wars must have had a severe impact on the production of scientific, artistic and literary works because of the elements of fear, death, sickness and poverty affecting the people involved. (I wrote that during a heavy thunder storm with a lot of lightnings making incredibly loud sounds and it is very difficult to ignore them and focus on your thoughts while the storm is going on at its peek so that is why I assumed that people who wrote during the wars must have written not necessarily during the bombings but before or after and they must have shortage of paper to write on just like everything else and I didn't have much either.) And also it is strange but one can feel the need or urge to go to the bathroom to take a leak when it rains or the rain can start after one goes to the loo. Do these have anything to do with one another? With this basic exemplary idea maybe something in the reader's mind might be triggered. Sometimes new ideas come out while reading. It might not even have anything to do with what we are reading. Actually one can even write without any reason to write at all. It can be done even just to strengthen the network of neurons in the brain as one draws new connections between the existing ones, making them stronger and creating new ones by using the eye, hand and brain coordination. Just like playing music. We do not necessarily play or make music for a specific purpose necessarily, we do it because we like it, enjoy making it and it is clearly proven now that making or playing music is one of the best exercises for the human brain. In a way it can be argued that there is a correlation or a connection or a similarity between the weather conditions and our thoughts. That must be why the term "A flash of inspiration" must have come out and that is why electricity has been associated with finding a solution or coming up with an idea.

It is usually illustrated in cartoons, comics and animations as a light bulb lighting up above the head of the character and many different versions of it are used in various parts of the world. That is clearly because thoughts occur as a result of electrochemical and therefore primarily electric currents that are generated in the brain. Actually, in order to remember or recall a memory the brain has to recreate the same electrochemical reaction that had been established at that moment back in the past. In other words data is not stored in our minds as they are archived in books and libraries. And the electrochemical signal has to be created in the synapse which is the connecting point between the neurons which is a nerve cell that carries information between the brain and other parts of the body in order for a memory or a piece of data to be remembered. It is more like a recreated memory. In case of a failure of a synapse between the neurons to transmit the signal, the connection is lost and the activity of remembering does not take place at all or is not entirely as expected, which is bound to increase, as we get older. That is why it is common to observe the rise in forgetfulness as people age and in some extreme cases it can reach a point where it is diagnosed as dementia. It is quite amazing that there seems to be a similarity between the electrochemical reactions that take place in the brain and the lightnings in the sky. It is also very strange that the terms some cultures have related to remembering or recalling or coming up with an idea and the lightning were being used in the language way before this scientific discovery about the brain was made. The reason I wanted to bring this subject up is because of the fact that cinema and poetry have the capacity to activate such extraordinary electrochemical reactions in the brain and therefore it has the potential to release and trigger new, unordinary and very rapid connections in the mind. Cinema has the ability to create thoughts and emotions almost as fast as they are created in a dream. There are similarities between dreams and cinema.

We dream individually yet we watch films collectively. They are both usually experienced in the dark. Of course films, as part of a mass communication system, have an influence on our conscious mind as well as our subconscious. It has been discovered that our eyes move while we dream, because of that fact they named this specific dream phase as REM, which is the abbreviation for Rapid Eye Movement. It is also revealed that the movements of the eyes correspond to the movements of the eyes in the dream so if the person looks in a certain direction in his or her dream the eyes of the person also move in that direction in the dream state as they are sleeping. It is known that the information and daily experiences are organized and archived in the brain during sleep. Yet it is really very interesting that our eyes move the same way as they do in the dream. Could it be possible that we are really seeing the dream? Dreams have a poetic quality because of the fact that they are generally not linear or realistic in the sense that they are usually abstract in terms of their flow in time and space. Narrative mainstream movies are mostly linear. In other words even if there are flashbacks and flashforward or different kinds of jumps in the stories they do not disturb their overall linear narrative structure. Events are edited in a typical, traditional sequentially ordered manner with specific parts such as the beginning, middle and end just as in most kinds of prose such as novels and stories. In poems and dreams you do not have to have such a linear narrative structure. The ideas, images, symbols, characters, spaces, time and events in other words almost everything is in free flow. Therefore there are more poetic dreamy elements in most of my films. Because their poetic dreamy structures are intended to give the opportunity to our minds, thoughts and emotions to be at a heightened level of intensity and refinement that they deserve even more of.

Especially mainstream movies, TV shows and series try to appeal to the general average audiences as the primary target group therefore they tend to oversimplify and make the storyline shallow or superficial, thinking that a less complicated and plain ordinary montage strategy and narrative will attract the attention of the public more. This is something that does not allow the full potential of cinema to come out and flourish. Action movies as well as all the others which facilitate fast editing, a lot of effects, fights, explosions, running and chasing scenes try to affect the audience by deliberately attempting to stimulate the senses in an intense way by focusing on getting a reaction such as shock, horror, fear, suspense and a rush of adrenalin. Romantic movies, emotional movies and sad movies usually try to touch the sense of loneliness deep down, the urge to fall in love, emotions and the feelings of pity generally aiming to make the audience cry or at least try to motivate the spectators to get into a sentimental mood which later usually turns out to be a happy ending. Horror and suspense movies attempt to achieve different reactions in various ways in order to trigger fear and suspense in the audience. In a way, these genres basically try to get certain emotional reactions from the spectators by pushing different buttons to activate specific emotions and instincts. It is possible to call this the exploitation of the primal instincts, impulses, intrinsic physical and mental reactions. They hope to make a profit and achieve commercial success at the box office by generally underestimating and simply underrating the capacity of our brains to the point where they ignore it's potential and treat it as if it were just a primitive mechanical contraption that is only capable of experiencing basic action and reaction based emotions and thoughts. It is not necessarily art or especially the true ingenuity and real celebration of cinema to attempt to artificially induce specific basic feelings by utilizing uncreative and unproductive, dull methods and techniques, taking advantage of the easily manipulated senses and the vulnerable human psychology.

It is not only an understated deliberate misconduct but also not much of a contribution to the essence of cinema either. (I am not trying to argue that they are all shitty movies that are full of crap, although a lot of them are. But I am saying that maybe they do not mean any harm intentionally but they cause a lot of unnecessary traumas for no good reason to some of the people who watch them and they do not play a great role in the development of a healthy psychology of an individual nor do much for the progression of cinema in general by playing with primal instinctive reactions of the senses with artificially created manipulative stimuli except maybe for some editing techniques, visual effects and some of the classics such as some of the films of Hitchcock who was a kind of an exceptional "psycho" himself considering his problematic and demented relations with the actresses according to his biography. We can not deny that there are brilliant, legendary suspense and horror movies, yet that is usually due to the exceptional talent of the director and the metaphorical, political, ideological or social messages of the stories in those movies. Some of those directors in my opinion would be Stanley Kubrick, David Lynch, David Cronenberg and few others but we must accept the fact that one's opinions can change over time, depending on the circumstances and the information we are exposed to. The banal or stupid jokes in comedy movies do not help the improvement of cinema as an art form either, even if they spend millions of dollars on them unless they make you laugh just like in some great comedies such as Charlie Chaplin films or "The Party" [1968, directed by

Blake Edwards with Peter Sellers as the main character] which can make you laugh even if you are watching them alone.) To get back to the topic of certain genres such as horror and suspense movies, I would like to make sure that there is no misunderstanding about my statement because there can always be exceptions. Besides the fact that they are consumed by the masses and regardless of their commercial appeal to large numbers of people at the box office, in general we can say that most of these kinds of movies are bland examples of cinema reduced to its most primitive form. The audience does not necessarily go on a mental journey just because of the fast pace of the editing or the intense visual effects. They all just sit there staring at the screen in a passive state far from any kind of intellectual, creative or imaginative activity. They are lost, disabled and paralyzed in the hyper-intense visual cluster and noise, unable to think in an emotionally stable, positive or productive way because they are deprived of their inventive potential. Unless they lose interest in the movie and fall asleep or get distracted and start thinking about other things while looking at the screen yet not focusing on what is playing on it. This happens while reading a book more than while watching a movie. The reason why we can get distracted while reading and start day dreaming is because we sometimes stop decoding the information in the book if it is not interesting enough or if we can not concentrate on it at the time. Yet since cinema offers audio / visual information directly without having to be decoded from written words we tend to connect with it visually and cognitively much easier than we do with literature or books in general. In other words not only do they feel more stimulating in the sense that they activate more senses simultaneously, such as seeing and hearing, but they therefore also feel more "real" in a way, and that is why we get engaged in them more attentively than we do with books where we can tend to get tired or bored of decoding the letters, words and sentences. That is why the biggest technology companies are moving towards 3D simulation but at the end of the day we are not designed or we have not evolved in that way, where we will end up having to wear all the simulation goggles or glasses or helmets and they will defect our vision both physically and psychologically.

The world of poetry and dreams are similar to abstract painting in the sense that they tend to let the imagination flow and liberate the mind. By their nature they are flexible, constructive, liberating, creative, innovative, abstract like poetry (except for certain types of poems which have specific rules) and they embrace values and qualities such as inspiring to imagine and being capable of embodying all emotions. Yet I must admit that there are dreams, poems and abstract paintings, which do not have any of these qualities, therefore, I must say that I am describing and defining them according to their structural potential and capacity. To make it short; free verse is more inclined to unleash the mind, provoke the reader to make one think differently, to criticize and to imagine more than most of the prose which on the contrary sticks to the regular, ordinary storytelling techniques as in short stories and novels because they use abstract concepts and images to make one go on intellectual and dreamlike journeys where one's mind learns to imagine by making new undiscovered connections in one's head.

Of course this statement does not encompass everything as I had clarified before. This is only valid for "good" poems I suppose in a manner of speaking. When I was thinking about poetry I made the comparison between writing poetry and someone who tries to fly like a bird knowing that he or she can not fly and thought that the psychological and physical struggle against reality and gravity is pretty much similar to writing poetry. By the way some narrative films, novels and stories can have the qualities of a poem and can be more poetic than most poems. I am trying to write in a way that is suited for rational comprehension therefore I will keep on track and avoid metaphors as much as possible for now in order not to confuse anyone. Yet there is one more very important subject about the speed of audio / visual information (data) and writing to be addressed. The speed of writing or speaking is always slower than the speed of thinking. Because it involves the process of coding that is necessary to turn thoughts into words. The thoughts must be transformed into visual symbols such as the letters that form the words, which make up the sentences and while talking the same thing has to be done to transform them into sounds. But the speed of thoughts and dreams is much faster. Because it does not require any transformations or coding, it just happens directly. In other words it might take a very long time to write or tell what happened in a dream yet ideas and dreams occur instantaneously. In short, since it doesn't require coding into another medium cinema can travel at the speed of thinking and dreaming. Cinema can literally travel at the speed of light and it can make us travel in time and space. I wanted to incorporate all of these ideas into my film as well but since they are quite complicated, difficult to translate into the audio / visual medium and since they take a long time to explain and visualize they are hidden in the backdrop or the background of the stories because otherwise they would have made the film extremely long. Many of these ideas I summarized and used to build the backbone, the skeleton and the infrastructure of the project.

Instead of explaining everything one by one I preferred to refer to the context where the stories are taking place in the film, which are parallel realities as implied in the inter-titles and in the synopsis. Most films present the foundation or the basis of their theory if there is one and the concepts and elements, which they build on to the foreground. I decided not to do that. Right when I was sitting at the same place that I am now, (at the time when I was writing the manuscript of this text I was) contemplating the film and in general about life, nature, reality and cinema there was an abandoned ship in the distance. I thought about shooting the first period scene of the film on the deck of that ship. I rented the costumes and bought some wigs from Istanbul. We shot the scene with two different formats both in 16mm and digital video. I operated the cameras and did the cinematography myself as I usually do.

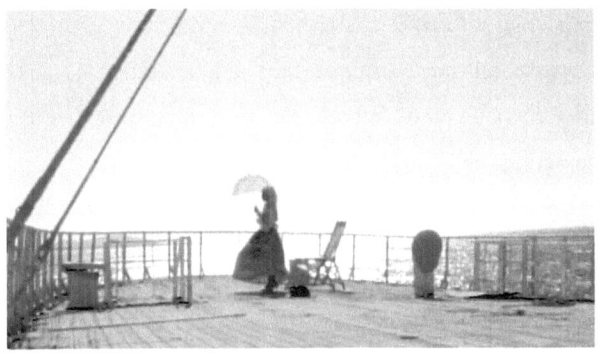

People write their memoirs or autobiographies when they are retired or old but I would rather do it now than later because as time passes inevitably we tend to forget the details and even if we don't forget them, they do not seem to be as important to us anymore over time in most cases and you know how the proverbs or sayings go "A stitch in time saves nine" or "Don't put off for tomorrow what you can do today." (To be honest I hadn't heard those before but they are in the dictionary.) Actually they might not be important for others but as it happened in this case when you row against the tide and try to make a complicated feature film without a budget, a producer, a production crew or any technical staff, professional lighting equipment, professional actors or anything at all, and if you complete it after many years without anyone expecting it to be ever finished, then it is a different deal because all these little details might turn out to be important in the future. At least they might mean something in a way as a road map or as a guide to some other people who are planning to make a similar effort. In other words, telling the story about how it was made allows one to understand the circumstances it was made in, which brings out the value and significance of it because otherwise people might assume that it is just another film that was produced under normal regular production standards. The same thing is true for everything and everybody reflecting the unique merits of the stories they have been through. Back to where I left off about that first scene in the film, I needed a deck chair for the deck of the ship. Back then there was a cafe or a small patisserie around where the ship was located and they were nice enough to let me borrow one for a while. Thanks to them for letting me do that. It was very hot. My friends who were going to act in this scene put on their costumes in the demolished captain's bridge of the abandoned ship. Maybe today nobody would come out all the way there to help a crazy project like this on such a hot day but they did and thanks to them for showing up. It was quite amazing that we got that shot.

I am glad that we filmed it right then because shortly after the ship was towed away from there. It is crucial that when you find an idea or a location you film them right away in independent, no budget productions like this one. Because if we hadn't filmed it right then we wouldn't have had the chance again, since we couldn't have had a deck of the ship built as a set for the film and that is one of the major differences between these kinds of films and the big budget movies. This is also the case for a lot of other locations we filmed at. After a while they disappeared. The blue telephone booth that we see in a later scene was transformed into or replaced by a giant daisy. It is quite sad because a lot of the locations and places in the film that we could show and say "We shot this or that scene over there!" are gone now.

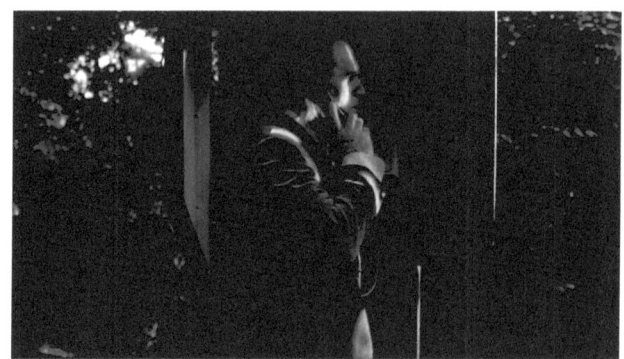

This subject matter is one of the subtexts of the film as well. The deletion of memories due to the destruction of the urban and natural environments. There are some mainstream movies about similar subjects but I have thought about it and we did make this film before they came out and they are not exactly about the same issues. This is something that attracts my attention quite a lot nowadays. They take the themes of some low-budget, art house films and turn them into big productions and mainstream blockbusters. I have also realized that they steal a lot of the experimental methods, techniques and aesthetic elements for popular movies, TV series and commercials as well. But we see them filching ideas and stories more often. I suppose it is easier to steal from the poor. Yet there are also a lot of examples of such, which do not necessarily involve low budget films. For instance, "Wings of Desire" (1987) by Wim Wenders was an inspiration for a Hollywood movie titled "City of Angels" (1998). Chris Marker's legendary film "La Jetée" (1962) was adapted into "12 Monkeys" in 1995 by Terry Gilliam. (This one made a reference to the original.) There are so many of these kinds of examples. Some of them take the main idea or concepts from other movies and interpret them differently and transform them into a different version of the story. The image of the person being connected to the machines with cables was originally one of the first to be presented in the anime, based on a manga, called "Ghost in the Shell" (1995), which was recently remade. This idea behind the image and the story was used in "Matrix" (1999) and many other movies. This is a strategy that the capitalist system uses in almost all industries. It takes ideas and parts of avant-garde, progressive and reactionary approaches of the opposition or the cultures of the minorities and by internalizing the concepts or the products even if they are totally against it, it turns them into commodities that can be consumed and uses them to its own advantage. In most cases they do not even care to make a note of the original or refer to the films they took the idea from and market it as if it is a brand new product, movie, idea that they just came up with. It acts like a big cell or a balloon that encompasses everything including its opponents, turning the original ideas into icons, brands, labels etc. as if they invented them, to be served as a part of the popular culture by hollowing out the original and corroding the genuine revolutionary essence of them in order to vomit them out in new packages without even paying their respects by at least referring to the original as the source of their inspiration.

I had mentioned that cinema as an audiovisual language can be as fast as thoughts and dreams, which I should expand on more. Most mainstream movies use fast editing for the action scenes, the fights, explosions and such, but that is not what I am talking about. By the speed of cinema I mean the potential speed of the free associative capacity of the mental activity during abstract and poetic creation and expression. What they usually do is nothing but a part of a kind of commercial marketing strategy or scheme, I should say, to get the attention of the viewers by showing action packed explosions, fights and effects forcing viewers to secrete adrenalin to keep their attention. That is the most primitive and basic way of utilizing the power of cinema and degrading it. Yet multi-million budgets are spent on them. Although so much money that is almost equivalent to the entire budget of some countries is funneled into these mega productions, unlike what one would expect, which is for them to be perfectly mesmerizing but unfortunately they are not, and they are full of unacceptable editing mistakes and so forth. It is possible to accept that a low or no budget film might have some mistakes and errors but it is not possible to understand how these multi-million budget movies end up having so many mistakes despite the fact that so many people work on them and an even more mind-boggling aspect of this is that they make it to the big screen with all of those obvious errors, without anyone catching them and having them corrected. Maybe they just think that nobody would see them, but they are clearly wrong about that. With such huge investments and unbelievable amounts of money involved one would assume that these movies should be worth as much as spacecrafts, airplanes, ships or cars, because they cost just as much, more or less, and that each and every frame of them are being examined just like any screw, bolt and nut on their financially equivalents but apparently they are not at all. It is an entirely different deal when there is need for a stuntman because those are scenes that you may not be able to avoid mistakes or mismatching edits. For example, in Terminator 2, when the terminator acted out by Arnold Schwarzenegger is helping the kid to get away from the liquid metal terminator guy, he passes the truck and grabs the kid with one hand, yet if you pause the shot or watch it very carefully you would see that this is an entirely different person. Another striking example, that doesn't probably involve any stuntmen, which makes it harder to explain, is in one of the Batman movies titled "The Dark Knight Rises" (2012) where Batman drives through the waterfall into the cave yet we see the car dry in the next shot. And it is not because of some special feature that the superhero car has. It is a loud and clear mistake. What actually really blows my mind is the fact that there are so many of these kinds of movies with a lot of mistakes and they are being made with super big budgets, with very famous movie stars acting in them, directed by very famous directors and with the help of the very best experts, technicians, crews working for them.

(I had started writing in Turkish but I changed my mind about the language I am going to write in because there are more English speakers than Turkish speakers and many of the terms I will be using are English. So I translated the part in the beginning that I had written in Turkish and added it to this part, which I have written in English.)

To return back to what I initially had intended to do, which is to tell the stories about the making of the film, I will return back to that but I will also sometimes reflect back on some of the subjects that I find interesting or related to the topic. I had been looking for an old car like the yellow New York cab and I had tried to make the streets out of cardboards with enlarged print outs of the facades of buildings clipped onto them. It was a bird's-eye view of the street with the papers falling from the sky, so I cut little rectangular shaped pieces of paper to use as the papers pouring from the sky as the toy yellow cab passed. Everything was black and white except for the cab. I also made the street and the pavement out of architectural model-making materials. It was difficult to make the cab go straight. Assistant students helped. Many thanks to them. It was quite crazy and complicated because we had to shoot the scene in slow motion on 16 mm film. Two assistants were dropping the little white flakes, which were the pages in this scene and a friend and another assistant were winding the yellow cab toy and trying to make it go straight. It was very hard to synchronize and before each take we had to pick up each and every single flake of paper from the model street. It was insane but that was the best idea I could come up with, since we could not shoot it on a real street and with a real car, yet we tried that as well, which I later transformed into a video installation with the footage from the real scene of the car and the papers. We collected all the papers from the street after shooting and we made the screen with them by hanging them on fishing lines and on to those we projected the loop of the papers falling as the car passed. It all did work out well at the end. Thanks to everybody who helped. Unfortunately I had to cut it out and use another shot for the scene because we couldn't find the exact same car in real life.

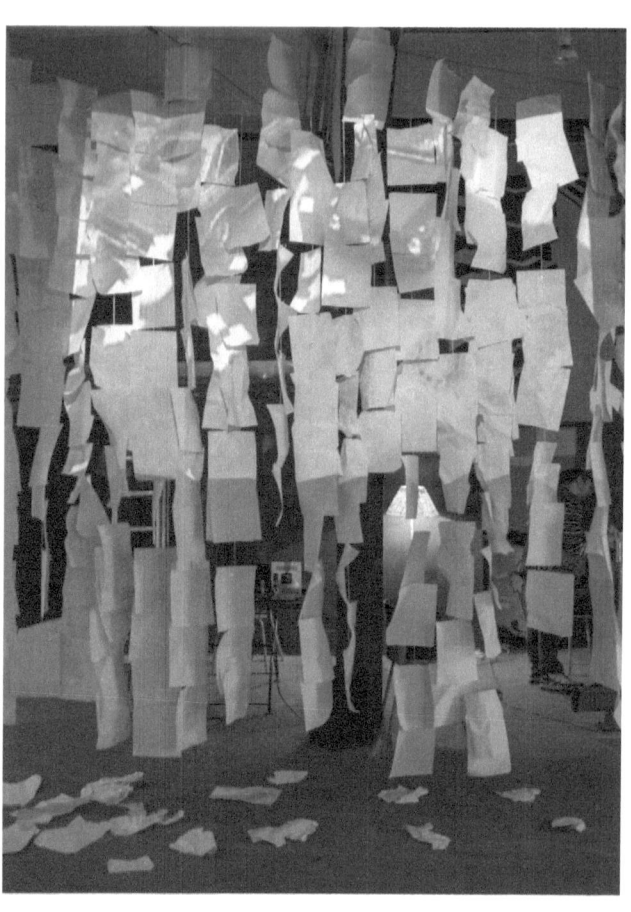

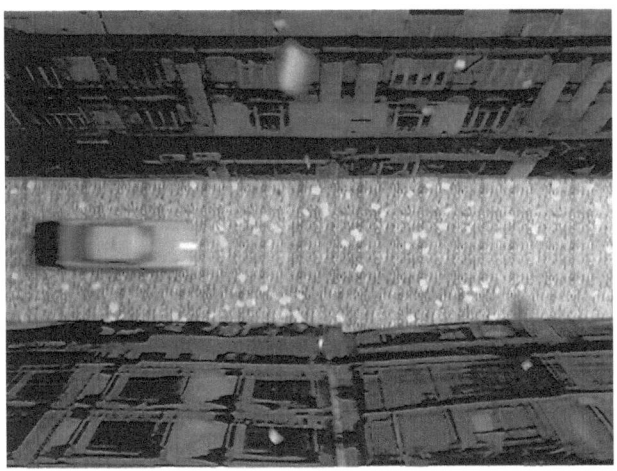

This is another very important difference between the industry and the independent, no budget productions, because I, as the director of this film, could change a lot of the things and scenes even add and cut out as much as I preferred, whereas a commercial production would usually restrict the director. Even Orson Welles said that he would not make another film with the Hollywood studios because they want to interfere with almost everything. In other words, if you are working with producers, studios, etc. they usually think that they own you and the film project, and therefore they, think that they have the right to step in and almost direct alongside you because they are financing the production. They have to approve every decision that is made because they want to make sure that the money spent on the film is going to be worth it. Therefore the director of an industry production can not experiment much and she or he is not allowed to change the script, the story or the main structure of the film in general. They expect the director to follow the script word by word and shoot each scene as illustrated in the storyboard. In my case I could do anything but I had to invent ways and come up with ideas to make the film the way I wanted it to be, but with a multi-million project you would just tell the production team to find a cab that looked the way you wanted it to look and they would either find one or have it built from scratch even. Since I didn't have money I had to explore different ways to tackle this problem. The toy car was yellow so that restricted me. To solve this issue I looked for some other old model cars and bought some small ones that would fit the scale of the model street we had built. I even tried to write down the number plate of an old car that was in a jazz festival commercial but the editing was too fast for it to be seen. I managed getting it after a few times but we couldn't track down the car. Well, it was clean and repaired so it looked like new but I wanted it to look old, dirty and run-down a little bit.

Some things in life, I suppose, happen after you have tried almost all the alternatives and failed. My suggestion is "Don't give up." because as in some other cases, this scene also got resolved by mere chance or coincidence. But as you might as well already know, some say that there is no such thing as chance or coincidence. One day I got out of my office at the university I was teaching at, after teaching some courses and editing some of the scenes I had already shot, and I decided to walk instead of taking the bus. I was taking the same route every day, maybe except for a few exceptional days. So I started walking up this hill, paved with cobblestones just like in the model street I had built, with old buildings just like in the model street too, and it was a cold winter day, if I am not mistaken. I saw an old American car. It turned out to be a black Chevrolet '55 with a white roof. They are usually with white roofs but some are entirely black and some come painted in different colors. But to make the long story short, I was mesmerized and shocked by this incredible coincidence. It was getting dark or maybe it was already dark so the streetlights were on. It would have been a great scene in a documentary about the making of the film to have the streetlight turn on right when I walked past the car in deep thought.

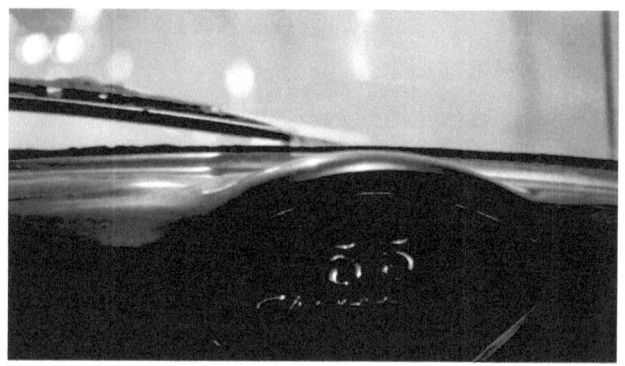

Anyway, there it was, but I had no idea about how to get in touch with the owner of the car, so I thought I would write a note and stick it under the windshield wiper and hope that it doesn't rain or that the wind doesn't blow it away at night before the owner of the car finds it. I looked for a piece of paper and a pen but unfortunately I didn't have either of them on me at the time, which was strange too because back then I used to usually carry a pen or a pencil and paper in my bag. Anyway I didn't have them so I had to walk up the hill to a grocery store to borrow a piece of paper and a pen to write a note. So I did and came back to where the car was parked. I don't remember exactly what I wrote but it was a small notepaper so I made sure that I wrote something brief yet convincing enough for them to call me back. As I reached for the windshield wiper I realized that there was a number on the dashboard so I wrote it down but I was hesitant to leave the note under the windshield wiper because some idiot could just take it and throw it away so I thought of an alternative where I would stick it on the driver side which was facing the traffic side of the street so that the pedestrians would not see it and interfere with it. In other words, the owner of the car would come to open the door to get in and drive off and the note would be right there above the key hole between the window and the metal part of the door. I had to make sure that he or she would see it, so I stepped to the drivers side of the car placed it right above the keyhole on the window and tried to make it stay there by sticking it between the window and the door but the gap was too wide so the note just fell right through the gap and disappeared in the door. So nobody would see that unless somebody took apart the door to repair the window or the door lock or something, but that was not likely to happen anytime soon and the note would not do any good if it were to be found years later. Therefore I had to go get another piece of paper and write the note again and put it somewhere where they would definitely see it so I had to put it under the windshield wiper or the side view mirror on the drivers side.

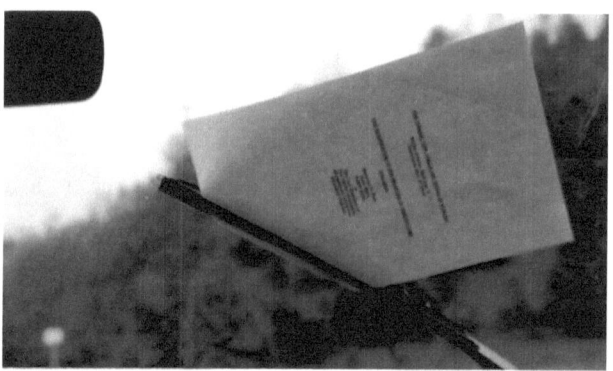

After the first disappointment this time it worked and the note stayed there apparently,

because fortunately the owner of the car called me the next day and he turned out to be a very cool and nice person, and it was another blessing that he agreed to help us out with this scene. We made an appointment to meet on a weekend at a location, which was not very far from where I had first seen the car. One of my students had the checkerboard pattern for the cab-look printed on sticky paper so him and another student assistant and friend of mine, Ömer Halifeoğlu, helped us decorate the car with it so that it looked like a taxi. Former colleague and lighting expert, Oğuz Yenen, had brought several cameras and a bunch of his students so we had a perfect time with at least five cameras and three cars including the Chevrolet '55 decorated like a cab. Many many thanks to both Fikret Yağan and especially Yüksel Yağan who let us photograph their car and helped us with the filming of that scene. I was very lucky that day. It was a long day of shooting in and out of the car and in the tunnel, where we were very fortunate too, because not too many cars came while we were shooting. It is very important to go out and celebrate all together with everybody who helped and participated after especially such a special day. It doesn't seem like much on film or the screen when you think about it. The man stops a cab, gets in it, they take off and drive through a tunnel but it took so much effort to realize it. And I think that was a miracle as well, because it would have been so costly and hard to get permissions for it, and so forth, to shoot that scene under normal industry standard conditions. Thanks to everyone again for making that possible.

There are some points I would like to make about organizing and preparing for a shoot even if it is just one scene. It is very crucial to visualize the scene in your mind. Do not just think and plan out the scene but go over all the details about how, where and when you are going to shoot and what kinds of equipment you will need. That is if you are especially making the film with just a bunch of friends, assistants, students and people volunteering to help. Otherwise if you have professional production assistants and a crew, you can not necessarily rely on them for everything but you can request that they do the planning and you can focus on your directing and your actors. I don't like giving advice, suggesting practical solutions or giving tips about how to go about shooting a scene or making a film but I thought it might be a more efficient, less painful and less time consuming process, especially for those who are trying to achieve difficult goals regardless of the lack of money, actors and equipment.

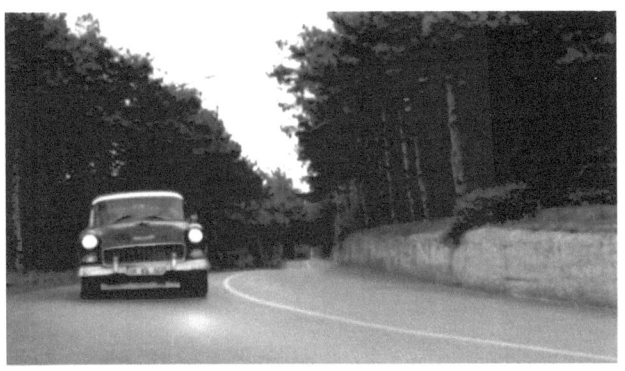

That is like comparing two entirely different ways of cooking. If you are an industry director, you are like the grand chef of a very expensive restaurant, where you have more than everything you need and want at your service: All the pots and pans, stoves, ovens, grills, all the cooking equipment and materials. On top of that, you have other people working for you. So that is clearly very different than trying to make a dish at home, without money, necessary cooking materials, professional people helping you and the ingredients you want. In this case you have to be extra imaginative, creative, innovative and positive. You also have to be very patient. The first case scenario sounds more desirable, fun and profitable, yet it is also definitely more demanding, stressful and painful because the owner of the restaurant is expecting you to get everything ready on time and demands a certain look and taste from you, therefore you are not really free. You are more like a high-paid and ranked slave to the establishment, than a creative artist in the kitchen. Many of the film students, and also oddly, many or most of the film scholars, professors and film theoreticians do not recognize this fact or they prefer to pretend that they do not know about it. This is a major problem for cinema and especially for the young people who want to study film and make films but they are not provided with this crucial information so many of them might be choosing the wrong path for themselves without knowing. For example, a student might apply for a school that is focused on training people for the film industry, where they are going to be expected to fulfill certain technical demands, yet the student might be more artistically inclined and he or she might be interested in the medium of cinema from a very different creative, experimental, artistic perspective and being misplaced into the wrong environment might harm or destroy his or her interest in cinema.

The opposite of this situation is also possible. Someone who wants to work as a technician or a specialized crew member or as a commercial director can also suffer from the opposite kind of situation where the university expects the film students to be artistic, open minded, experimental and creative. Therefore it is very important to do the research to find the right kind of school, college or university to attend, because it can change your life for good and radically affect your future. It is like giving a patient the wrong medication or feeding your dog or your pet the kind of food that they shouldn't be eating. The outcome or the results can be deadly. This is true for all fields of study, all the arts, humanities and sciences. If a person, especially at a very young age, is forced to comply with a certain approach to something that does not agree or fit in with his or her mind's chemistry, or with the way they prefer to see and approach, then the result can be, and usually is, very destructive and bad. You might ask how one can know without trying. That is also correct. If you do not know your inclinations, potentials and choices then I suppose you will have to try and see. That is what experimentation is about. But it is also very incorrectly interpreted, especially in places like Turkey, where most people are ignorant about experimental cinema, but before getting into that subject

I would like to return back to the difference about the commercial director and the no budget filmmaker. Since this crucial distinction is not known to many of the theoreticians and people who are acclaimed to be film professors, historians and scholars, they approach the image on the screen as the creation of a totally independent and free artist's work, yet in most of the cases it is not true.

There are many factors that go into the realization of the idea, the production, post- production processes, which we are not aware of, but those factors influence the direction of the film. Even if the studios or the producers let the director to be totally free, which is not the case as I have explained before, there are millions of coincidences and random factors that can not be estimated or known because when we are watching and analyzing a film we are only looking at the image and the story yet we are not aware or informed about the bigger picture where there are accidents, sicknesses, unexpected technical problems, the weather conditions, the psychologies of the actors, actresses, the director, the members of the crew or the details about the equipment, the materials involved and so forth, therefore without that information the analysis of the film would not be based on the facts involved in the process of making the film but just what appears on the screen and it can be very shallow compared to the bigger picture of the story that took place behind the scenes. That is why film studies and almost all the books on cinema approach the medium without the background analysis and they sometimes, or even in most cases, focus on issues that were influenced by external technical or other factors as if they were intentionally and deliberately placed there in the film. Therefore, they usually end up misinterpreting many of the aspects of the film, assuming that there were not any mistakes, accidents, technical difficulties or acting and directional errors based on physical or psychological circumstances.

They turned to take a man made medium and study it as if it were made by God, without any influences or mistakes. It is a very common problem that we face, not just in cinema but in all industries and fields of study. Men and women make mistakes, yet almost all products such as cars, knives, TV remotes and even airplanes and space rockets are designed without enough attention on this matter, except for the airbag or the black box, but those are not necessarily enough to save peoples lives once a mistake has been made. For example, there is the eraser for erasing the mistakes we make while we are putting our thoughts, ideas and feelings into words, so, that basically, on it's own, proves that the humankind is equipped with a brain and body that makes mistakes. Therefore, we should focus on this fact more than we do and consider it for all the arts and sciences to have a safer and more reliable approach. In other words, although a piece of art might be at a higher level of perfection and inspire emotions which trigger an enlightening vision, we must admit the fact that nothing that is man-made is perfect or flawless. Even if it were it would still be challenged by time. This is not to say that one should not try to exert the highest degree of effort to accomplish something in striving for perfection, yet deep down one should also know that it is not possible. This is the one and only or maybe one of the ways of getting the closest to challenging a task that is considered to be impossible.

All big thinkers, artists, inventors, scientists, game changing pioneers have come up with ideas and inventions and all sorts of things that changed the world. The things they achieved were incredible, especially for the time they were living in. These new ideas changed the way people live. Today we take most of the technology we are surrounded by for granted but they did not exist some time ago. If you look at the history of the civilizations you can clearly see certain inventions and discoveries that changed everything. These can be considered as the game changing steps of the evolution of the civilizations. Fire, the wheel, the steam engine, the assembly line, the car, the plane, the spacecrafts, the atom bomb, the Internet, etc. and many more discoveries and inventions changed the way humans live. Some of them killed millions of people and all sorts of living things like the atom bomb. The invention of the car and the plane changed the way people and things travel around the world, therefore it also changed the way business is done. Cinema is an invention that changed the world as well. It is one of the biggest industries around the world. It is a very complicated form of art and entertainment, which has the potential to influence the way people perceive and the way they live. This is an incredible power. So how can we understand more about how it does this and about it's components. First of all we must realize that the film industry and the art of cinema are not necessarily the same thing at all. As I have mentioned before the big chef in the kitchen of a luxurious restaurant is there to make certain types of food that taste good and look good so that the restaurant owner can make money and profit from the food that the chef makes.

This is to say that a commercial director is expected to do the same thing in the film industry. The same story goes for the screenwriter or scriptwriter. They are expected to write stories that will sell. So we can not necessarily say that it is pure artistic and creative vision and talent that is motivating them to produce work. That is where we can clearly see that the studios, producers and other businesses which are investing in the production have expectations from the films they are investing in or sponsoring, therefore they try to develop strategies to make sure that the films they produce make it big at the box office and sell well on other distribution platforms. This is a very important factor that damages the artistic and creative potential of cinema. We can also understand that the studios, producers and investors prefer not to just give away the money, hand it over and let the director do whatever he or she wants to do with it. There has to be a balance you might think but I am not sure if such a balance is a good idea for an art form to exist freely and independently. The money people, meaning the people and companies that will finance the project, look at it as if it were any other product that they want to sell, so the idea is to make it as cheap as possible, make it in such a way that the audiences around the world will find it interesting enough to make an effort to watch it. The director in that situation is in a position where he or she has to make sure that the film achieves that goal which is set for the film as any product in the capitalist system. Yet in many other cases this is not the only strategy and the goal. Some films with unbelievable budgets strive to distribute certain thoughts, ideologies to manipulate the views of the masses around the world.

They sometimes try to do this in a subtle way and some others do it obviously without trying to hide their agendas. For example Rocky and Rambo were not laid-back in their stories and they were directly set out to influence or change the views of the people about political issues. They both fought the USSR, as a boxer in one and as a soldier in the other. There are so many examples, you can guess which ones so I don't want to make a long boring list of those films because they would fill up pages for no good reason. Yet the other kinds of more subtle films in terms of the storytelling strategy and structure can be even more dangerous or effective because they do not tell the propaganda of the film right away or in an open, clear and direct way. They sometimes even use subliminal codes and messages to manipulate the mind while it is unconscious and certain parts of the brain without the audience realizing it. So some of these kinds of productions (films and TV series & shows) intent to brainwash the spectators without them noticing. But they are not obvious about it. So the majority of the audience, or maybe none of them, understand what is happening. They do not understand what is going on. Some people argue that it is possible to control the minds of other people. It seems to be possible with the help of hypnosis. I suppose some scientists also agreed that films could be used to accomplish such a task. Actually it might be true because people watching TV or a film in the cinema look like they are hypnotized yet for that to be a proven fact the brain waves of the members of the audience have to be tested and direct unconscious response of the spectators must indicate that they are obeying the instructions just as it happens in hypnosis sessions. It is a scary thought. I would hope and wish that it is not true and that it can not be done yet there are instances such as the paralyzation of the entire group of Japanese children watching an animation in a movie theater. Maybe it is an urban myth but the ideas that Freud's nephew Edward Bernays came up with truly shocked and shook the capitalist society at a major scale. He is the father of capitalist public relations, advertising, commercial strategies and many more, which evolved to be the biggest tools, used for worldwide propaganda strategies. He took Freud's research about the subconscious, the ego, the superego and the id and turned Freud's theories into a weapon in order to market and sell pretty much anything including ideas, views, ideologies, products and all sorts of services almost worldwide because he had realized that according to Freud's theories the human mind could be manipulated to the degree that it did not act or react or think rationally. So the ego was unstoppable and he could take advantage of this lack of control that was inherent in the human mind and use it to promote, market and sell anything. If the image of a car were to be presented with a sexually attractive and desirable female and a comfortable, economically satisfactory family image, the male consumers would do anything to have it even if it sounds irrational but the capitalist American life style is based on this hypnotic strategy.

Without Bernays we could have not known Freud because he made him famous as a scholar in exchange for using his ideas to turn the entire world into a crazy capitalistic consumption machine. According to his strategy if an idea, product or service (whatever they may be) were to be presented in a certain way, the human brain would be triggered almost automatically to want and desire whatever is being presented and he or she would buy it even if they do not need it at all. Many cultures were facing a massive agenda that was created in the US. and it has come a long way transforming the behaviors of societies around the world. It doesn't make sense but that is a fact. Commercials, ads, PR methods, marketing strategies and many films play a very big role in this audio-visually stimulated hypnosis. To return back to my film, "For The Blinds", some of my students said that it is mind-boggling and that it is a vast criticism of the media. Many people who watch it say similar things. That is because it is true. In the light of some of the information I shared with you as I used to do also in my BA and MA level lectures, I did not utilize the commercial techniques to manipulate the minds of the spectators but I wanted to show them a version of our possibly futuristic reality and by making metaphorical references to things that are connected or relatively similar to our lives and reality I hoped to inspire people to think about what is going on and what is happening to us.

We usually do not have the time to stop and think about many things that are happening, so I wanted to take this opportunity to help the spectators in the audience to stop and think about the reality we are living in and where the recent technological developments the social, cultural, economic and political circumstances have brought us. I did not intend it to be a vast negative criticism that is depressive and I don't think that it turned out to be so. I simply wanted to draw attention to some fundamental questions and problems, which we tend to deny, forget or prefer to be unaware of. On the other hand I do not want to sound pessimistic about the future or the commercial film industry in general because some interesting films are coming out and many more good films will be made. So that shows that the industry has some open doors for interesting, philosophically deep and emotionally mature, well structured, aesthetically pleasant films with beautiful cinematography sometimes as well but I suppose when the studios and the producers interfere with the content of the project in order to make sure that they make money at the box office, they usually end up ruining the film or finance intellectually less sophisticated, even stupid and badly made films. Or they take a good idea or a well made film and turn it into a lame, shallow movie that stinks while they are gutting out the original idea's or film's unique qualities, hoping to popularize the concept and make it easier and more attractive for the masses.

In one odd example Wong Kar-Wai was requested to direct an American version of his film "In The Mood For Love" And this film is also famous for its improvisational direction, meaning it was not strictly shot according to a script. Actually it was also argued that it did not have a script at all. So the director and crew improvised with the actors and actresses on the set, which is not a common industrial approach at all. The results of all of that totally experimental production turned out to be a great success. The cinematography was beautiful, the acting was great. So the studios in Hollywood asked him to make an American version of it in the States. It was titled "My Blueberry Nights" and it ended up being a very bad movie. In even such a case where the director is the same; when he was brought to work with different actors, actresses in another country, at a different location and setting, it did not work. I felt the same way about Haneke's "Funny Games". The original European film and the American version are almost identical except for the actors, the location, even the story is exactly the same but for some reason something doesn't work. It just doesn't feel right for some strange reason. I can not explain why exactly, but you can see it. Maybe even if the director is the same and the production budget is provided from different places, the places where they shoot make a dramatic difference. It is kind of like as the saying goes "You can not bath in the same river twice." One of the reasons why I brought this issue up is because I tried to do something similar in a way but I did it without knowing and in a different way. My intention was to experiment and see where and with whom I could get that effect, the cinematic composition, the dramatic quality that I wanted, so I shot many versions of some of the scenes. Some I never used at all because they did not work the way I intended. Sometimes the acting was bad, sometimes the lighting was not good enough. Anyway, that is always the case. Every production shoots more than what they need because there is always something that doesn't work out exactly as desired. That is why there are many takes of the same shot or the scene. To get everything right you usually have to shoot a couple of times. In some cases this can get out of control where the director demands more than ten versions of the shot. Nowadays, after I had come up with a different approach to this problem I realize that some blockbuster movies are also trying to come up with methods to cut down their working hours and shooting time by showing the same things over and over again such as in the movie called "Edge Of Tomorrow" (2014) where Tom Cruise is a soldier in the future and he keeps living the same things like in a computer game. He dies and starts from the beginning. It is quite annoying I think, because you end up wasting your money and time watching the same scenes over and over again. I am not quite sure why they did that. Maybe the actors' shooting schedule was too tight or maybe the production couldn't afford to pay for all the stars' scenes so they ended up repeating the same thing over and over again to cut down on the money and the time. I actually did the opposite and emphasized the parallel realities by showing the same occasions in different places and times.

In other words, I intended to compose and juxtapose the images in the composition of the frame and also in the editing in such away that each time a person watches it the compact imagery and complicated structure of the montage would allow the viewer to realize different aspects of the stories and the premise of the film. That is one of the reasons why it took such a long time to complete. The scenes and imagery are designed to motivate and encourage the spectators to dwell in the film as if it were a dream and some of the people who watched it said that they felt like they were in a dream. The reason I wanted that quality in the film is the fact that we are free of the rational, standard logic of reality and liberated from the limits of our cognitive mind in the dream state, therefore we can imagine and witness fantastic, surreal, illogical and fairy tale-like unbelievable things while we are sleeping. I think freeing the mind is good for the soul. Because I would like to think of all the souls as part of an eternal entity, which might be nature on Earth and ultimately the universe. When we think about the problems and issues we are bound to focus on and the issues we have to face and live with, it becomes clear that our souls and minds are capable of doing a lot more than just struggling with the circumstances we are surrounded by. In other words, we

spend our days and lives trying to survive. We have to
work to make a living, to buy food, to rent our homes
and to take care of our children, yet there is one very
clear point I would like to make, which is that survival
should not be the ultimate goal for our bodies, minds and
souls. Of course, we do not choose to live like this.
Actually, we are forced to live like this. Time is the most
valuable thing in our lives because we all know that we
are all going to die some day, sooner or later, but we
forget about that fact in our daily routine. Instead of
doing the things that we would like to be doing in our
limited life span we lose track of time doing whatever
makes the boat float; meaning, in a way we waste most
of our time working in a company or doing some job that
pays the rent and feeds the kids but it is not how we
would like to spend our time if we were presented a
choice. So in a way we are imprisoned in our little lives
because we have to earn money to survive. But if that
weren't the case, what would you be doing or how would
you like to be passing your time? I have thought about
this equation while I was making the film. Money equals
time plus effort. Big productions need a lot of money
because they want to get things done in a very short
period of time, therefore they have to buy the time and
the effort of the people to make them work for the film

and get it done quickly. I did not have the money so I spread the production over a long period of time and since I could not afford to pay people to work for the film I did almost all the work, and as I mentioned before, my students, friends, family and volunteers helped me out. That is the case for most independent films I suppose. The concept of time is very important in our lives. Because that is pretty much all we have and we have to decide what to do with it before we pass away. Most of the people do not have the luxury of being able to choose.

In other words, I want the audience to continue imagining even after the film is over and during the experience of watching. In order to give an example from the film I will go back to the investigation scene where I am sitting dressed as a security guard or policeman eating a cheeseburger in front of the monitor. I ended up shooting the scene on my own, so I had to coordinate a few different pieces of equipment such as the camera and the DVD player. The scene is composed of two frames in which there is the security guard sitting in front of the security monitor. It is shot from the side, and the monitor turned towards the camera gives a feeling like a split screen but it was all shot in one take, meaning the scene that we see in the monitor was playing real time as I was filming. The shot on the security monitor shows a doctor played by Prof. Adolfas Mekas, a nurse and the patient in bed. It is a deformed dreamy setting with asymmetrical black and white tiles. It is a long shot, which required a lot of work. I built the set and painted it. There were some clouds on the walls. We had brought in a three or four storey high scaffolding and I had placed the camera on top of that to get a higher angle which helped to imitate the angle of the security camera. We also shot the scene of the party in the same studio. I shot those scenes on 16mm film with a BL camera (a model that TV news channels such as BBC used back in the day) with a 400ft. magazine (the film holder on top of the camera). It was heavy equipment. The other shot that we see on the monitor was shot in Halle, Germany, so in one composition I brought three different places into one.

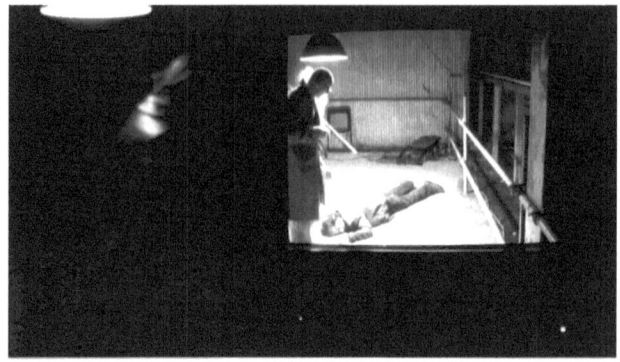

One being the hospital scene shot in New York. The torture scene of the bold detective walking around a man lying on the floor, face down, whom I acted as well in Halle, Germany. The broader picture or frame including the monitor also shows the security guard sitting in front of the monitor so that brings the fourth dimension into the scene, which I shot in my apartment in Istanbul, with the other black and white scenes that were playing simultaneously on the monitor. The party scene was a difficult one as well. We brought kegs of beer. We told people that it was a costume party. I asked my artist friends to bring their paintings and other artworks. They hung them on the walls. I had an installation with an armchair and a TV that I had painted white. There were bands and DJs playing music. Cops came to shut us down but I told him that it was a scene for my film that we were shooting so they left. That was amazing. Friend of mine told me that that was the best party she has ever been to. I think it was the best party I've ever been to as well, so I am quite proud of that. Yet the only problem was that the guy who had given me the film stock had told me that he had not shot anything on it and that it was totally unexposed, but unfortunately there were some parts where they had shot some footage. They were very underexposed so you could not see clearly but some shots l had to cut out where they were more visible.

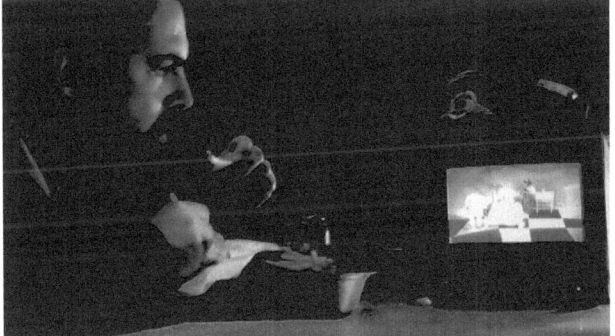

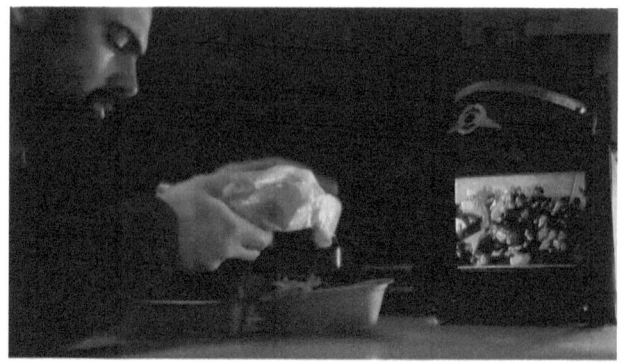

(When 1 started writing this book I was writing in Turkish. After a couple of pages I realized that it would be better if I wrote in English because the potential reader for this book would be English speakers more than Turkish speakers, most likely. So I switched to English but later I realized that I would go back and forth between the two languages sometimes which could be a unique quality about this book because they are usually in one language or another. Yet most people would think that there is a mistake and they would stop reading once the language changes so therefore I will stick to English and try to translate the sections that I wrote originally in Turkish.)

Uzun zaman önce filmle ilgili bazı fikirlerimin
pekiştiği bir yere tekrar geldiğimde bir senaryo yazmayı
düşündüğüm filmin yapılış sürecini ve bu süreç içerisinde
ve sonrasında aklıma gelen bazı fikirleri kaleme
almaya karar verdim. Bu aslında filmin çok önemli
bir baş yapıt olduğunu düşündüğümden değil. Aslında
yaklaşık 15 yıllık öğretim üyesi olarak film dersleri, atölye,
seminer verme ve konferanslara katılma sanımı oldu.
Sinemayla ilgili düşüncelerimi ve deneyimlerimi kaleme ve
öğrencilerle paylaşmaya çalıştım. Bu nedenle bir filmin
yapılış macerasını yazarak bir bakıma genellikle imkansız
olduğu söylenen bitmesiz, parasız ve olmasa olmaz diye
adlandırılan birçok zorun olmadığı koşullarda yapması olan
bu filmin yapılış hikayesini sinema öğrencilerine ve film yapmak
isteyen birçok kişiye farklı bir perspektif ve ışık tutabileceğini
umarım. Bunun gibi sinema dersleri verilen sinemanın
şire benzediğini ve dolayısıyla film yapmanın da şiir yazmak
gibi öğretilemeyecek bir şey olduğunu düşünüden ancak yapılabile-
ceğini kendi yapıtlarımın ve akademilerimin üzerinden tecrübelerime
dayalı fikirlerimi paylaşmak ve bu yapıyla da bunu yapmayı

umuyorum. Sevgili hocam Prof. Adolfas Mekas film çekmek, yazmak
şiir yazamamız gibidir. Sinema yapmak çok pahalı olduğundan
ve işin sadece kağıt ve kalemin yeterli olmasından dolayı bunu
söylerdi. Bir bakıma haklıydı da insanların çok fazla şiir
okumamasından dolayı şiir sinemaya kıyasla çok daha az kişiye
ulaşıyor ancak bu şiirin veya yazının daha hızlı ve fazla ve
anlatı alanı olduğunu gösteriyor. Halta yapılış yerine kelimeler
ile bir bakıma hayal gücüne daha fazla fırsat tanımaları bakımından
soyut anlatıma ve dili daha çok anlamaya yardımcı oluyor. Şöyle
bir şiir sinemada deneyselliğe ve zamanın dokunma filme
benzer. Kelimeler düz anlamında, alt bir bulgular eksilme
ekmek roman ve hikaye gibi edebiyat türlerinde olduğu gibi
sinemada da kurmaca film yeni genellikle ayrı sinemasında
egemenlik kurmuş olan sinema türünde kaçırımış olan bu
anlatım biçimi çoğunlukla düz bir zamansal anlatı içerisinde
geri ve ileri bazen atlamalar yapmak izleyicilerin daha kolay
takip edebilecekleri ve kişiler. Şimdiye kadar birçok popüler
roman ve sanatsal film türü olduğundan sürecl, soyut şiir deneysel
sinemadan daha yaygındır. Şiirde olduğu gibi deneysel sinemanın
sözce kendine has soyut bir anlatım, evreni gerçekleşerek izleyeyi
bir bakıma özgürleştirmek ve hikayeci hızlı ve gerçekçi bir
anlatıyı doğrulamak yerine izleyicinin ayrı şiir okuması gibi
imgeler arasındaki bağlantıları kaplamdan doğru dışlayıcı düşün şiir karşımızda
yapmanın sağlayarak izleyici kendi anlamını oluşturur.

Translation of the Turkish text:

I was lying down on the couch, listening to the radio with my eyes closed. There was a crazy drum solo playing on it. It is amazing what one can do. Actually everybody does pretty incredible things in their life. Many things that we don't care about or take for granted seem to abound in our daily lives yet they are quite magical when you come to think about it. It is important to be aware of that. Because just as the day passes and ends, before we know it, without us realizing it our lives will pass and end in the blink of an eye. Time flies by and as one gets older it seems to pass even faster. Another thing that we should be aware of is the fact that I have started writing in Turkish instead of English. It must be because I think of certain things in Turkish and some others in English. Nevertheless, after this leap between the languages I am going back to writing in English and the things I wrote so far in Turkish I will translate into English but I will not translate directly word by word but write maybe even in an entirely new and different way. I might even write about totally different subjects.) It is quite unbelievable that I switched back and forth from English to Turkish and now back again to English I guess this aspect of this book would make it a pretty unique one, considering that not too many books switch between languages. They are usually in one language or another as you know. I suppose it is because we or I think about certain things in English and some other matters come to my mind in Turkish or maybe I just began writing without thinking about which language I should write in. I guess it doesn't matter as long as I am writing what I'm thinking.

I was writing that time is a very precious subject because we all know that we are born, we live and eventually die in one way or another. My concern is the fact that we can not use our time very efficiently. I was thinking that I wouldn't write everything I wrote in Turkish or translate it but I did. So as you can see everything changes over time. I'll move on with the essence of the subject. In short, I was saying that life passes in the blink of an eye just like a day in your lifetime and it seems or feels like time passes even quicker as we grow older. Anyway, I will not emphasize that because I know that it is an annoying fact. I would have liked to somehow make a little change in my life if I had the chance and I suppose I have in a very small way. For example, I was packing the projects of my former students the other day and I realized, or I should say remembered, how crazy it was and is that I taught for about almost 15 years and if we assume that there were at least 30 new students every year, which I am very sure was many more than that, the number of students considering the different classes I taught would add up to an incredible number such as at least 450 and I am sure the classes were much more crowded so that number should be around twice that, which would make it around 900 to 1000 students and that many young people are, I believe, enough to start making some changes. I think we all tend to underestimate ourselves and the things we can do. Except for the ones with a huge self-righteous ego. I suppose we do not have to be great historical heroes, pioneers, warriors or masters of sorts, or geniuses, but we all should know that we can have a purpose and even if it might seem too big or unachievable we should remember that all long journeys and triumphs began with a small step. Therefore, even if things do not work out, we must keep in mind that things change and we can change things, that we should not lose our courage and faith in whatever positive idea and good thought we might have. In my case, I was lucky, or maybe I should say, I should consider myself lucky that I had the chance to teach all my students because the small differences people make in a positive way in a person's life makes much bigger positive changes in the future. I hope that time proves me right.

Teaching is a very hard profession and it is very difficult to teach in general, especially considering the complexity and sophistication required for a complicated art form that demands a multi-dimensional imagination and a unique vision for the search for cinema. Besides the technical and theoretical aspects, the depths of the innumerable subjects involved in storytelling structures and visual aesthetics are very intricate matters to be thoroughly addressed.

By the way, by saying that we can all have a purpose I did not mean anything divine, holy or religious at all. We do not have to go with and agree with the holy beliefs or religious perspectives, yet at the end of the day, what I meant to say is that all people from anywhere can want to have a goal or purpose in life but not everybody has to do that. People can choose to just live comfortably, make a living, maybe raise a family and that can be their purpose, which is usually the case anyway. That is fine too. I don't have a problem with that at all. In fact, I would like to do that as well someday. Something very strange just happened. The radio station playing on the computer stopped all of a sudden and a weird message came on, saying "This radio station is not available in your country." repeatedly, so I got up and walked to the computer which is back in the study-room and as I approached it, it began to play again without me touching anything. The only thing I might have said was "Why did it stop playing all of a sudden?" It happens sometimes but I can not understand why it does because it is just another radio station on the Internet and why should it become unavailable out of the blue and go back to normal without me or anybody interfering with it. It must be one of those mysteries of the Internet.

Anyway, back to our story, I got a little carried away with that inexplicable event but to get back on track, although it was and is difficult to be a good, well rounded, meaning not just theoretical or just practical and technical instructor or film professor, I hope that my students benefited from my lectures, classes, seminars, workshops and advice because I realized that I spent a very long time teaching and it happened during the best years of my life, so I would rather think in a positive way and consider that period of my life as a kind of sacrifice I made, maybe not totally consciously at the time and not entirely intentionally, which might be interpreted in a wrong way, so I will clarify exactly what I mean in basic and simple words. I did not intend to be a professor or instructor or teacher. The university asked me to teach. In fact they wanted me to be a mentor to the students, so I accepted the offer. I did not think about the consequences or the future at the time. Year by year time passed and I found myself teaching and giving lectures for almost 15 years. I must admit that it was not always fun but I do not regret having done it. As a matter of fact, I would like to open a studio, a workshop space or a small place, which would be kind of a school or educational institution. It would involve me and maybe a couple of other people. That can be one of my temporary goals for now. It would be kind of a place where a small number of people come to draw or paint and there would be other art and film courses. Later it would maybe include some other subjects such as cooking, music, etc. The space would be also used for exhibiting the art and screening films. By the way, I keep returning to the idea of having a purpose in life but it is simply because many people die without the possibility to reach their goals or dreams and we have only one life to achieve them. It is going to sound kind of crazy but it is just like saying "Everybody is crazy but some are crazier than others." which means that not everyone is crazy enough to accomplish the goals that might seem unachievable. Therefore, we could say that some people might be more inclined for certain things, or if that sounds too fatalistic, we can restate that as, "Some individuals or souls are more determined, luckier, more persistent and dedicated to doing certain not easily achievable things."

It is not exactly like saying some people are prettier than others or some families are richer than others or as in the famous novel "Animal Farm" by George Orwell "Some are freer than others." You probably get the point I'm getting at. The probability of certain things happening is usually higher depending on the circumstances.

Therefore we can assume that if someone is good looking that means that he or she has a bigger chance of becoming a model or an actor or an actress. Yet it is not always necessarily true. Member of a rich family has a better chance of becoming successful because the family can afford to pay for an expensive education and they support their kids to move up the ladder in life. But the situation I'm talking about is not about that. It is about doing something that is not quite expected of you. Kind of like changing the rules of the game and doing something revolutionary, avant-garde, game changing, something considered to be impossible. Well, I will repeat my joke about this: DO NOT TRY AT HOME! that is the kind of situation I am talking about. I am sorry if this is starting to sound like a personal development book or something like that, but my intention is not to make it sound cheesy, yet many of those books people buy to develop their personality, become more successful people, tend to give ideas and lecture people about how they should think, live a dream to be "better", "more successful", "healthier" individuals. I do not like that. The world wants politicians with no campaigns, judges who are not rich. Neither film nor painting or any other form of art can resist time (as the material).

Sometimes I take short notes to remind me of certain ideas. The lines above are also an example of such notes. While watching TV, reading or just thinking an idea comes to my mind and I try to capture it and write it down. It can be very hard sometimes because thoughts occur to be very clear but it is difficult to choose the right words to express them in the right way in sentences.

Time has passed and I had to attend to a lot of different problems in my personal life such as moving and re-organizing my former students works etc., therefore I couldn't return back to writing for some time. It's quite amazing how much our minds are capable of. The circumstances and the surroundings are very important for our thought processes. For instance, right now I am writing under the candlelight because the power is out.

Electricity that we are almost addicted to makes us think that it always existed and that it always will, but we should not take everything for granted. In a way, not having the lights on seem to have a positive effect on my creativity and productivity. Let me share a few more details about the making of my film, which are directly related to electricity. The worst experience in writing or editing on a computer is when the computer crashes or when the power goes off and you do not get a chance to save your work. That has happened to me many times. It is really nerve-wracking. One other terrible problem with the editing and rendering processes is that the computer gets over heated, stops working or crashes. That is one of the reasons why I had to buy an air conditioner in order to get the film out of the computer. Well actually I had to have one installed at my office because I was constantly getting sick because of the central air conditioning and heating system but it also helps me render the film on a desktop computer that was not designed to handle heavy tasks such as rendering an entire feature-length film. So in order to do that I would turn the air conditioner to the lowest temperature, which was I believe 18°C, on Fridays and let the computer do the rendering during the weekend while the office was not being used. Sometimes it would work and sometimes not. It could not render and export the entire film as one file, so I had to export it in bits and reassemble them again as longer sequences. These technical details might not mean much to the regular reader who does not know about digital postproduction but I had to mention it as editing, rendering and exporting are some of the major elements and processes of filmmaking.

Power is a strange notion. One can not live with it or without it. I believe power, as the word we use for electricity, is one of the biggest problems in the production and postproduction phases. Since we depend on electrical circuits, lamps and computers, electricity is the most essential factor in both production and postproduction. Yet it is important to remember that many works of art, pieces of music were created before electricity was invented. Because the lack of power gives you the freedom to think and imagine differently.

For instance, a composer living centuries ago would sit in the dark under the candlelight and compose some of the most beautiful pieces of music. It is incredible. This is something to remember while listening to classical music. The word "Power" is a difficult concept to conceive. The other meaning of the word "Power" also indicates authority. That is another topic to discuss in terms of filmmaking or for any kind of creativity or production that involves more than one person. Power is a dangerous thing. For example, people in power, as in politics, have to be very careful because the decisions they make affect a lot of people. It is the same for a filmmaker as it is for a captain. You have to think from many different angles and consider many variables.

Flexibility is a virtue but it is not always a solution. Because most of the time one strives to achieve something specific, you know, a shot or a scene and it is not possible to get it right in the first take. So in many cases you end up shooting the same dialogue or a scene that requires almost perfect timing over and over again and it gets tiring for the actors, the workers on the site and the crew in general so if you give in and do not try a couple of times to get what you had in mind then the tension on the site would be less but you would probably end up having to use a bad scene or edit it out later. So it is very hard to keep a balance and control the power, because if you insist too much you might drive people crazy and if you don't, then you might not get what you want. So maybe the best approach is to plan ahead and rehearse if you can.

Another crucial matter is to make sure that people are having fun. Because people do not mind repeating lines or doing the same thing if they are enjoying it. The hardest part of the job is to keep everyone happy and to be able to give directions at the same time. Since I do not work with professional actors the set can sometimes get out of control. People make jokes and they like to fool around, which is fine because it brings in positive vibes to the set but if it gets out of hand then things can get pretty difficult, therefore I believe that the best way to solve this problem is to let them be and enjoy the experience and to try to keep the number of takes to a minimum so that people don't freak out and you do not end up with hundreds of takes. Back in the day when we were using 16mm film, I was filming with my Bolex camera and we did not need any power during the day because we didn't need lights and the camera you would just wind to get it to work, so we didn't need any electricity at all. Now the battery life and the space on the memory cards can become big problems while shooting. If a shot is really bad, it is better to delete it than to keep it, because you need that limited space on the memory card. When I am filming with film rather than video, I prefer to do the rehearsals with video so that I do not waste the film stock, which is very expensive, therefore very valuable and very limited. When you are working with film it is very important to use the film stock efficiently and in order to do that you have to make sure that everything is perfect before you shoot.

It has been quite a long time since I had a chance to write again. I had to move and unfortunately I twisted my ankle very badly so I had to wear a cast for 15 days which was very frustrating experience indeed. Now I can walk and that is a wonderful feeling. One becomes aware of the importance of very basic activities, needs and things when one loses them. We should never take anything for granted. Many simple things in life mean a lot but we are not paying attention to them all the time because we assume that everything will be the same all the time but unfortunately things tend to go wrong at some points in life and that is when we realize the significance of what we were capable of or what we had. That is why health and time are two of the most valuable things in life. This is one of the reasons why everyone, especially people who have dreams and goals, should take extra care of their health and use their time very effectively. Those are some simple but essential points that I wanted to make before moving on. One other subject I would like to discuss is about film funding and the selection of topics. In many cases we witness the funding of films, which are about humanitarian issues such as refugees or hunger or the discrimination against specific racial, ethnic or religious groups. And usually they are funded, meaning those kinds of themes seem to be getting the funding they need, yet the production crews or the directors who apply and get these funds are usually, or most of the time, from other places, different backgrounds, which have nothing in common with the people who are suffering from the circumstances. Something about that seems unfair, wrong and weird. This is an issue that I used to point out in my graduate documentary courses as well, because of the fact that since the beginning of the history of documentaries, people went to different parts of the world to capture the suffering, the pain and the injustice inflicted on other people. This is of course sympathized with because they seem to want to help those people by exposing their problems to the world, yet I have my doubts about how much good that does to the people who are suffering. Because it is similar to the situation where people are being shot at or dying and the journalists, reporters or the documentarians photograph or film the people who are being killed. This is a terrible situation and it always gets raised in ethics, journalism and film studies. Supposedly, they intend to raise awareness and by doing so we assumed that people, communities, institutions, organizations and governments would attend to the issue. I think that it would be more effective and helpful if they basically spent the money on the people who are suffering from the urgent problematic situation. It is sometimes difficult to differentiate between the honest and whole heartedly humanitarian people who are truly trying to help and others who take advantage of the situation and apply for the funds because it is a "hot" topic and because they will look good in the eyes of the community and the public by looking like they are trying to help the victims.

I think that it is quite sad that people try to take advantage of such a situation because it is almost like a connecting point between the previous subject of time and health. In other words, when time is running out and if someone is in danger, or injured, or threatened, or dying, one does not take a picture or film that person, post it on the Internet for help or try to get it published in the newspaper or get it broadcast on the media to get help if they really genuinely want to be somewhat helpful. I believe that a direct and immediate reaction would help that person or the people suffering from a bad situation a lot more effectively. After that, instead of sending film crews, giving those people the skills, the equipment, facilities, the education and the funds to make their own films and take their own pictures is okay, but only after saving them and making sure that they escape and survive the danger. I know that this may sound strange to some people but I believe that giving the funds directly to the people who are suffering from a problem makes more sense than giving it to some other people to make a film about the situation. That would be the ideal in my opinion, but of course the world does not necessarily want the best or the most ideal solutions to problems because then the conflict would be resolved and there would not be a profit to be made. It's actually very sad to be seeing that humankind in general does not choose to overcome poverty as much as it could be done. It's an undeniable fact that we could have already resolved all the major issues that the world suffers from such as hunger, wars, poverty, discrimination, global warming and many more. I do not think that it would be very difficult to do but it is a matter of choice. For instance, it is the perfect example if we look at what happened with Tesla's inventions. He made a car that did not need gas or anything at all. It ran on air. So it would have eliminated carbon emission and pollution once and for all, but they did not care about his invention and did not invest in it because they said that it would not make money. In other words, the solution to one of the biggest problems on Earth was found and the invention that would save the world was already discovered and manufactured but the capitalist investors did not find it profitable and therefore now we are facing global warming and pollution, which might bring the end of life on this planet. The same is true for poverty and hunger. So much food and energy is wasted. If the poor people were provided with even just a small percentage of the amount of what is wasted everyday, there would be no hunger or poverty. So, in other words, the solutions are there and they are absolutely feasible but they are not carried out because not enough profit would be attained. I can only think of one clarifying question: Does that make sense? After all, one can say that people are not rational creatures. I can understand that, but it is an eminent fact that money and profit are man made abstract representations and they have no real value when it comes to nature. Therefore having cash or making profit will not mean a thing when humankind ceases to exist and gets extinct from the face of the planet.

The values that we create do not exist in nature. And we can not eat money to keep on living. We need nature to survive. People seem to have forgotten about that long time ago and we need to remember it and get back on track to reverse the harm we have done before it is too late. Some people might think that I am oversimplifying, but I suppose one can not underestimate the heart of the matter, which is the fact that this is really a matter of life and death. So, in issues like this, one can not overstate the importance of either neglecting the danger humankind is facing and ignoring the rapidly approaching death and extinction, or simply understanding the undeniable urgency of the situation and doing the right thing to stop it from happening. In other words, if people of all different races, ethnic groups, colors, nations from all sorts of backgrounds don't join together to find and carry out environmentally friendly sustainable solutions to the most crucial problems such as global warming, poverty, wars, ethical and religious conflicts, pollution and many more, which I am not going to list because they are clearly known by almost everybody, it will lead to a very sad and painful end of the humanity as we know it today. It is also very interesting to see that humans seem to be unaware of the fact that our planet can get hit by a meteorite or an asteroid, which has happened before, and it wiped out entire species and almost everything that was alive on Earth. Therefore if we are intelligent creatures as we claim to be, then I think it would make a lot more sense to concentrate on the danger of getting extinct because of an asteroid hitting the Earth rather than anything else. If we were smart enough to realize that we are just one of the many kinds of creatures that live on this very beautiful, unique and precious planet and that there would not be a war to fight, nor a crop to cultivate, nor any water or food to drink and eat in order to survive if a comet were to crash into our world. So instead of fighting each other, we should be focusing on issues that are risks to our existence and our planet. It is very interesting that often, or sometimes, when I write or even just think about something the subject comes up in a documentary or a show on TV. Just like the other day, after I had written about the asteroids I came across a show where Stephen Hawking was mentioning the same issue. Therefore I feel that my idea is pretty much approved by one of the most intelligent and influential scientists of our time. And I assure you that I wrote my thoughts down and watched the interview on TV a few days later. It is a mystery, but it is true. Maybe we can call this incident a result of coincidence but in other cases it seems like a miracle or something magical. In other cases when something bad happens that can be called something like a twist of fate.

I want to get back on track and connect the dots. There are very strange occurrences, events that seem to be coincidences. Some are so unbelievable and odd that we think that they are miracles. And those magical things happen. We sometimes witness them with our own eyes, or we hear about or read about them in books. History is full of these weird tales. As a matter of fact, we might get to see one or experience some of these rare events ourselves in a lifetime. I do not think that they happen very often and that is why they are special moments. Cinema tries to imitate these kinds of concurrences using artificial lights, visual effects, sets, actors and actresses. That is one of the reasons cinema can be magical as any art form can be, but since it embraces time, it has that power of illusions because things seem to be happening in real time as we are watching. Theater has the same potential as well, but there are more restrictions due to the physical real presence of the stage and the set and limitations that come with that, yet in cinema you can edit two entirely different scenes or shots with entirely different angles together but in theater the audience is always at a certain distance and each individual spectator has a specific perspective or view of the events that occur on stage. Therefore it has more boundaries than cinema.

I would like to return back to the stories and events that took place while we were trying to make the film. I will tell this incredible story that happened in Barcelona yet it all started in Berlin. The reason I want to share this specific event is because sometimes the things that happened backstage or behind the scene are quite as interesting or sometimes even more interesting than the scenes in the film. I was in Berlin for an art exhibition. Some of my friends had moved there from New York where they had organized a big art show, which took place at the Metropolitan Building. I had built this sculpture out of recycled construction materials that I collected from the streets around the exhibition space. It was quite a big sculpture that looked like a rhinoceros yet it was titled: "I can't believe it's not a rhino!" Later, after that exhibition I was asked if I would like to exhibit it at another gallery and I accepted so we had to find a way to get it there. Thanks to my friends, they borrowed an old lorry that looked like an ice cream truck and we took the sculpture up to the gallery in that vehicle. It was quite an adventure. Anyway, after the show my friends moved to Berlin where they put together another art exhibition and a book. It was called: "Overkill". And they invited me to be in the book and the show as well. While I was there a very strange thing happened. My friend from Spain, whom I went to college with, Roger, told me that he had some very close friends staying in Berlin and that I should meet them. One night we went to a party that was taking place very close to where we were staying. It was right around the corner. So, as we talked and met more people it turned out that this apartment was right across from the loft where my Spanish friend's friends were living and they happen to be at the same party. That is one big coincidence but that is just the beginning. I bought a Russian 16 mm camera while I was there. I asked my friends, whom I had met there, if they would like to help me shoot one of the scenes in my film and luckily they accepted. So we got some costumes, hats, etc. translated the dialogue in the scene into Spanish. It was going to be the scene where a half naked woman enters the loft where two men are sitting and conversing.

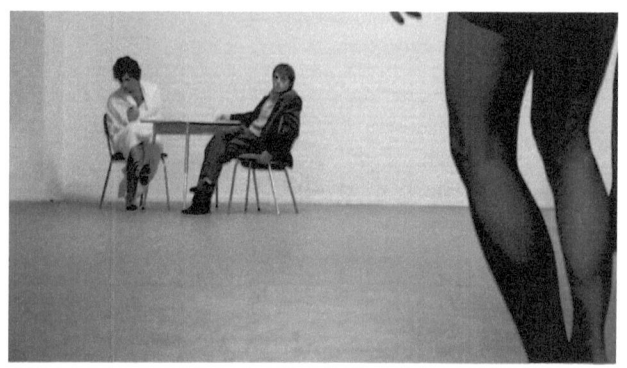

The male characters are Seintn and Pweg and the female character who comes into the room is Levos. Anyway, to make the long story short, we shot the scene and also another one where the detectives interrogate a man they have captured. I used my Bolex that I had traveled to Berlin with and the new camera I bought there to shoot the scenes. And one of my Spanish friends whom I met there, Dionis, was recording with his digital video camera. Later I took the film to the lab to get it processed but something had gone wrong. It was not exposed properly or maybe the x-ray machine at the airport had ruined it. I don't remember all the details but I had returned back home and started teaching at the university. I asked my friend if he had the original video of the scene. But then, there was not any way of sending big files over the Internet like we do now. He said that he still had them. Right around the time one of my works got accepted to a big international exhibition, which was going to take place in Madrid, Berlin and Paris so I filled the forms to travel and participate at the conference, and seminars, which were taking place alongside the exhibition. I went there and also took the fast train to Barcelona where my friend had the tapes. We met and had a great time. A friend of his joined us. I think he was a painter. We went to the beach, after a while my friend gave his jacket to his friend. He put it on. And I think it was the same jacket that he was wearing in the scene we had shot in Berlin. His friend got really drunk and started talking like a mad Spanish poet of some sort and eventually got up and walked into the water. The cassettes were in the pockets of the jacket he was wearing. So the only remaining footage of the scene we had shot in Berlin were drenched in seawater in Barcelona. We ran and got him out but it was too late. The tapes were soaking wet. It was a terrible accident. I had lost all my hope for saving the footage and the scene, yet fortunately we dried them and they worked. So there you go. Now if I hadn't written this story would you have guessed that those images had traveled across countries and had gotten almost destroyed in the sea in Barcelona? It sounds like a crazy story but I assure you that it is true. Therefore it is almost a miracle that this scene is in the film now. Many events seem to happen at random yet when one thinks about it some unusual chain of reactions or coexisting occurrences attract one's attention. For instance, if we analyze the reasons or the conditions, which led to the formation of a specific event in life, as simple as anything such as people running into each other on the street or a major event in history, we are irresistibly compelled to somehow link the occurrences that happened previously. Therefore, by doing so, instinctively one tries to draw connections between different and separate pieces of information. It's almost the basis of our perception of logic. We are inclined to try to make sense out of everything that happens and even draw rational conclusions based on our awareness of such coincidences, events and our own personal experiences.

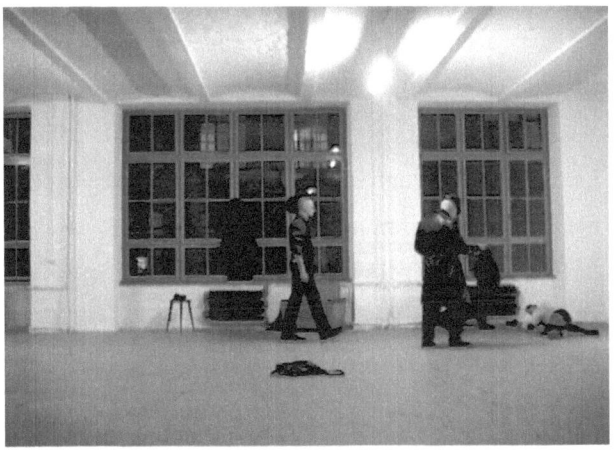

Some people prefer to call it "An act of God" which is perfectly understandable if you always refer to the Gods or God in order to explain inexplicable events such as natural disasters, rain, fire, the sun, the wind and the rainbow as a chore of the Gods or God. In other words we turn to keep God or the Gods responsible for things that happen which we can not explain until one day maybe science comes up with a rational explanation. I might have mentioned similar ideas about this issue because the thinking and therefore the writing process requires one's thoughts to spin in a spiral where the thoughts and ideas form a platform or a spiral shaped path that passes through many different physical and spatial variations in order to reach there, almost indefinitely multiplying permutations and infinite number of conclusions based on other imaginable probabilities and possibilities. Actually these issues are all intertwined and deeply related; therefore we would not be severely sidetracked if we were to discuss the connections between our thought processes, natural events and acts of creation. These are the very same elements that play a crucial role in writing a story, a script and making a film. It is also true for dreaming, imagining and writing poetry, yet those require a different state of mind and an entirely different liberty in the patterns of thoughts and connections of bits and pieces of data. I call that "abstract thinking". We need a bit of both for a good piece of work, whether it be a film, an artwork or a piece of literature, and in whatever form or format they may be.

Returning back to the events that took place in Barcelona, I must admit that I personally have not been able to come up with a logical or a scientifically rational or spiritually understandable explanation. But if I had not shared this memory about that scene and how it got dragged in seawater, people would have probably thought that it was one of those scenes a scriptwriter wrote and a director shot. Just one of those ordinary scenes that you get to see in a movie. In other words, if I didn't write these memories nobody would be able to know the facts behind the creative process. And by doing so, I intend to bring the stories behind the scenes back to life in order to open the door to a new layer of occurrences, stories, events and paths which will take us to many more possibilities in our thoughts. In other words, there are many levels of thinking and trying to understand a scene or a film or an artwork, because as in this specific case, there is the scene in the film, which holds one or more stories in itself, and then by introducing the thoughts, events and coincidences that went into the making of the scene, many more layers and stories are revealed and that is very important in this case because as l said before if the unknown occurrences behind the scenes were not mentioned, then people would not know about the dangers, the accidents, etc.

that we had to face during the process of making the film. They try to do something similar by editing in the unused shots in the credits in commercial films and especially comedies, but that is not exactly what I am trying to do here. You probably already see the difference. Anyway, to make sure that I get my point across, I would like to refer to a technical aspect of filmmaking: Back in the good old days, people had to struggle with the difficulties of making a film with film, because there were no digital devices back then. However ancient it might sound to the new generations, that was not a very long time ago, since I can remember it. The computerized filmmaking came out about 20 years ago or so, because I was studying at Bard and everything had to be done on film, which was very difficult, compared to what we have now. It is almost like child's play to make a digital film on a computer compared to making a film with 16 mm or 35 mm film. That is why it is very important to know about the backstage of a production and the technical aspects of making a film. That is one of the main reasons why I am writing this memoir. People tend to assume that all the technology we have today existed since the beginning of time, which is completely false as we all know, but when it comes to reading and analyzing films, I guess many people forget that aspect and fact. First of all you had to deal with a physical and chemical material called "film" which we referred to as "film stock" if it is unexposed and "footage" if it is exposed and processed. Now these terms are almost all forgotten. I don't know if any school teaches film, using film anymore. In my experience, I was the only professor that I know of who had sufficient hands on experience with film as a material. I taught film courses for more than fourteen years and to my knowledge nobody had any experience with film as a material nor knew anything about film as a material including all the older professors. Therefore they did not know anything about how to make a film with film, which is a very intricate craft and art in itself. This is a very crucial matter and it is unbelievable that people who had no experience with film can teach film. It is very odd in my opinion, because many aspects of the technical mechanisms, the chemical processes and the very fact that the material of film having its own language comes with its materialistic and physical properties. For example, you have to make very precise decisions about where and when to cut. There is only one right frame to choose to make the cut from one angle to another in most cases, so you have to examine the shots separately and find the frame where the cut must be made and there are many technical limitations such as having to use a Moviola or a viewer or a flatbed which are different equipment you have to use to magnify the image on the 16mm film, which is tiny therefore it is almost impossible to see the details in the frames of the shots with your bare eyes. To make the long story short, it takes a lot of craftsmanship and hands on experience and a lot of hard work to make a film with film. I will write about those technical matters as needed yet what I'm trying to address here is the fact that the experience of working with the physical material or film makes a whole lot of difference and it is a very difficult craft besides being an art form. You can not make mistakes. If you do, you might have to forget about the shot or the entire scene sometimes. For example, if you run the original film material, which is your footage, through the equipment too many times it gets scratched and that is why you see those lines on some old films. It can even happen on the first run through the projector. I lost a lot of scenes and shots like that. Some got eaten, meaning got jammed in the machines, some got scratched to the point where I could not use them. In other words, film is a real thing and it has its physical existence. It is not like the digital file in the computer that you can cut a million times and nothing happens. It is not an abstract, virtual, digital video file but a real physical material with a soul I'd like to say.

My point is that all the coincidences, events that happened during the planning, meaning the writing and all the pre-production process, has an influence on the outcome as much as the ones that take place during shooting and editing. If I hadn't come across that car or the actors and actresses they wouldn't have been in the film and maybe the film wouldn't have been completed. If the tapes were damaged by the seawater in Barcelona, that scene we had shot in Berlin would have been lost. Since they are there in the film I suppose we are living in a nicer and definitely much luckier version of how things could have been, considering the bad things that could have happened.

Speaking of versions I like to work with different variations and versions. I did that with my short film "ZYMOTIC - AMAUROSIS" for which I drew and wrote many different variations of the shots and scenes and taped them on one another as layers of possibilities. So you could open the little windows, which were made up of cut out pieces of paper taped onto the pages of a notebook. One optional shot or a scene was drawn on each piece of paper illustrating the action, the characters and the composition of the shots presenting the sequences of alternative ways to approach the cinematography and the narrative structure. I do not think that it is a very common method. Actually I might be the one who first came up with that idea. It was absolutely a multi-layered technique for writing a script and drawing a storyboard. Anyway, in order to reconnect the idea of working with multiple versions and variations of stories and cinematographic presentations I would like to return back to the source of the story which is one of its basis in reality. That short film, which I shot on 16 mm, was about a virus in the eye that could record visual data. The theme of the film was a little bit complicated so I will not get into the details but the reason I brought it up is because I ended up having a virus in one of my eyes, which was an extremely rare case in medical history. So, to cut to the chase and to make the long story short, one must consider the possibility of what one imagines, thinks and creates becoming a part of one's reality. Some say that if one wants something to happen very passionately then it is more likely to happen. So bear in mind, when you are making a film that it might actually happen to you as well. Be careful what you wish for, as they say.

Most of the commercial films have happy endings. That might have something to do with the fact that music, films and art in general directly affect the human psychology. If most films ended badly or in a sad way then the possibility of the number of people who suffer from severe depression, melancholy and similar states of the mind caused by sadness would most definitely increase. That could lead up to more suicides. In that case it is not just us, meaning the individuals who write, create, compose, draw, paint or direct, but all the people who might come in contact with our creation who are at stake. Because the mood we create or the feelings and thoughts or ideas we deliver with our films or with whatever form of art we make, we can influence the people who watch them or come into contact with them. Therefore, although it might sound strange, we must be aware of this responsibility as writers, composers, artists and filmmakers. The energy and tone and mood of our imagination and creation have an important influence on the audiences and the people in general.

To make it sound less didactic I will say that they might have an effect on the psychology of the people. Therefore it is always better to keep that possibility in mind. What we think of, dream about or imagine can become real. Hopefully that is clearly why we start off by thinking and planning before we do something or make something. Our brain focuses on an idea, plans the actions, materials etc. required for that specific idea to become real, and then executes it. Writing the ideas or drawing the sketches are the preliminary stages of planning which is the core of the creative process that eventually leads up to the production or the realization of the dream. As a matter of fact I believe that writing is one of the most magical aspects of our potential as creative thinking creatures because it might be one of the most distinctive abilities of the humans. All the animals do pretty much all the things that we do but I do not think that there is one creature on Earth that reads and writes besides the mankind. That brings us back to the idea of coding and decoding which has been the basis of many philosophical arguments in the social and cultural studies, which obviously includes media studies as well. So in other words, we have been trying to express ideas, thoughts and feelings with different methods since the caveman. They drew animals and other things on the walls of the caves they lived in, in order to code a thought by using symbols, which resembled the animals, or things they were trying to express. Others would see it and understand what it meant. That was the beginning of the basic communication skills and the messages we can still interpret today. So we can admit that it is efficient enough since it still works. We do not clearly know why they went through the trouble of drawing those big animals. Who knows, maybe they used the cave walls to remind themselves or one another about something that they had to do such as hunting that animal or something just like we do by writing notes and putting them on the refrigerator. So, as a joke we could think of those drawings as notes of the women in the cave to remind the men to go out and get some of those animals because they were running out of food. Just like we do now to remind each other about the groceries that we are running out of. That is just a funny interpretation, but why not? The reason is important of course but the fact that all humans feel the urge to express themselves in one way or another is essential. Since nobody can really argue about that, we can move on from there. No matter what form of art or language we use it all comes down to the same primal instinct, I suppose which is to communicate what is crucial for the survival of the humankind.

I will try to draw your attention to the fundamental issue about making films after having made some points clear about the evolution of communication, language and arts. This subject that can be analyzed further in detail but I do not want to get sidetracked. The core of my argument is the fact that expression and communication are inherent desires and among the prehistoric needs besides eating, sleeping and reproduction, which are the primary physical activities necessary for the survival of most living things and most animals. So why do we need this humanly expression? Or artistic expression? First of all, because I believe that it is essential for survival. The manifestation of our souls is possible through our realization of freedom. In other words if we were forced to express certain thoughts and feelings but prohibited to express our own ideas, thoughts and feelings then we would feel imprisoned just as it happens in dictatorships. It doesn't matter if it is fascist, religious or capitalist. When one is under pressure not to express certain emotions or thoughts then one can not be free yet I also mentioned that our feelings and ideas which are reflected in our work, such as a film, music or novels, having the potential of becoming real so which path are we supposed to take when we are creating? The issue is clear, yet it is also up to you. Are we always supposed to think of good things and make our films about good things so that they become real and the bad ones don't? I am not quite exactly sure about that but having had such bad luck with my ideas becoming real I must be more careful I suppose. Because it might not be true for everyone but based on my personal experience I must say that I should take this matter most seriously. It might sound stupid or unrealistic but as they always say about approaching a project, you should base it on your own experiences or ones that you can relate to, which I personally have never done or recommended, yet in my opinion it can work the other way where if your films or novels turn out to be similar or the same as reality you should stop and think well before doing anything and especially before making your next film. It is a very difficult position to be in if that were the case. The reason behind the difficulty is mainly controlling the fast pace of the thought process in the mind. One very crucial aspect of cinema that I have tried to address also previously is the fact that film is a medium that is capable of reaching the speed of thought and imagination. In other words the images that appear on the screen can somehow flow close to the speed of light, which is very much related to the potential of cinema being able to transmit information as quickly as it happens in the mind. Therefore cinema can be thought of as a time and thought machine that allows one to jump across time and space.

I must also acknowledge the fact that cinema is also a mood machine, meaning that it can change your mood or the psychology and the emotional state of the audiences. That might sound like a general statement but the least I can say is that it has the potential power of changing and manipulating the feelings of some of the spectators in the audience, if not all of them. So to be more scientifically correct and precise, we can say that cinema has the capacity to be considered as a "Mood / Emotion Shifter" as well, just like music is in many ways. Songs have the same kind of effect on emotions.

Before I move onto another story about the shooting of a scene in the film I'd like to mention the reason why I did not have a chance to write for a long time. To be honest with you, I must accept the fact that I made somewhat of a "time travel". The airplane was invented by the Wright Brothers right around the same time as cinema, and they both had an enormous impact on human life on Earth and civilization. An editor, Walter Murch, who works for big Hollywood productions, talks about this interesting coincidence in the history of groundbreaking inventions. I used to show that documentary about cinema and the film industry in class. Anyway, to make this long story short, right when I left off writing about cinema being a *"Time Machine"* I actually experienced a very similar experience where I got on an airplane and flew to New York after so long (after almost 20 years) and it really felt exactly like I had traveled in time, because a lot of things have changed since I left. The people, my friends, places and the entire technology had changed and I couldn't even recognize a lot of the streets or places I used to live around. I guess that is what we could call *"Time Travel"* and now I am back at the same spot where I started writing this book, looking at the same pool where we shot one of the scenes in the film.

I had also mentioned the time when I had the idea of shooting the opening shot of the film sitting at the balcony here. So it is interesting how, when and where things start, develop and end. I intended to finish writing this book here at the same spot where I started it. Now I am looking at the pool where we shot the scene of the man acted by myself, lying on the surface of the water, face down and the voiceover in the film says: *He thought that he was dead... but he wasn't.* That is the scene where there is a long pause between the first half of the voiceover and the second part, because seeing that the body in the water is not moving we assume that the person is dead but then he pulls his head out of the water so the audience realizes that he is alive. It was a difficult scene to shoot because there was just me and my mother at location, therefore I had to show my mother how to start recording the scene after I composed the shot and framed it the way I wanted it. Then I ran down to the pool, which is about 100 m, or so away down the hill and got into the water very slowly so that I wouldn't make rings of waves around the pool. I asked my mother to press the record button on the camera and let my self down into the water. I had to inhale as much air into my lungs as I could to stay motionless for as long as I could to make myself look like a dead person floating on the surface of the water.

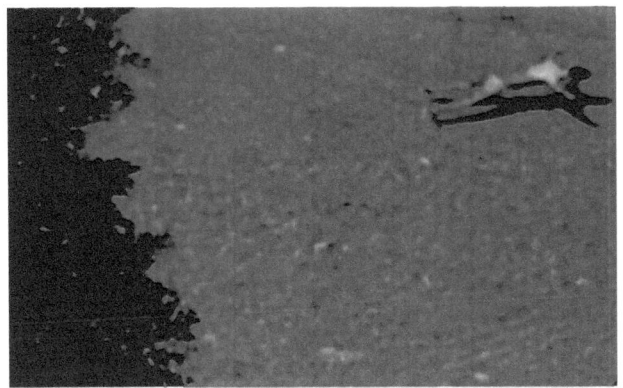

It was hard because since I had clothes on, my legs and feet would sink into the water and my torso and head would float on the water so it took us a few times to get it right. Thanks to my mother for her help and patience. Come to think of it now it must have been a torturous experience for my mom because I was asking her to help me shoot a scene where I was acting as a dead person floating in the middle of the pool. It probably was not a pleasant thing to do yet she appreciated the film when it was completed and came to almost all of the screenings of the film at the museums and at the festival, which made me very proud and happy. It is amazing what our mothers do for us and we can not pay them back even if we tried very hard because the effort and patience parents give to their children is immeasurable. The second closest person for someone growing up is probably his or her teachers or professors. It might not be similar in various other ways but that is what most educational systems around the world intended it to be like. We can not call our teachers or professors when we run out of money or when we get into trouble but they're intended to be figures out there that help us, teach us and support us in that sense. It is not their responsibility to nurture their students as if they were their nannies of course but they are meant to be there for the students to be able to learn from them or to be looked up to. Therefore being a teacher or professor also requires a lot of effort and patience. Sometimes more than the parents, considering that they are not there for their own children but for other people's children. The reason I wanted to bring this topic up is the fact that we usually do not realize the importance of having our parents and our teachers until we lose them. I felt like I lost a member of my own family when I heard that he had passed away and I could not hold my tears when I recently visited Prof. Adolfas Mekas' grave on Bard campus. He was a very special soul. And I am very lucky and proud that I met him. I would like to share a memory with you that involve both him and me. We had a moderation system at Bard where you would have to pass a kind of examination with a presentation of your work after two years of studying and you were not allowed to continue studying at the department if you can not pass it, so it was very important. I had asked some musician friends of mine to play music while I read the narration for the soundtrack of the film. Back in those days, it was very difficult and expensive to make a film with a soundtrack because you would have to cut the sound on 16 mm sound stock, which was magnetic tape. You would have to synchronize the sound with the image. So you would have the spool the film, mark the in and out points of each sound on the soundtrack, take notes for the mixing to be done at the lab and the sound studio and you would merge the sounds together on different wheels "rolls" if you wanted to have multiple tracks and then you would send the film to the sound studio to have the mixing done according to your notes with the specific indications about the frames where you want them to take effect. Then it would be sent to a lab where they would lay, or in other words write the optical soundtrack on one strip of film, which would be the one and only screening copy or the final print of your film because all this process took very long and it costed a lot of money which I did not have. I was on a scholarship when I was studying at Bard. That was, I believe, given to me based on need and my portfolio, which was wonderful because otherwise I couldn't have studied there, therefore I couldn't have had the chance to meet Prof. Adolfas Mekas and be his pupil. Anyway, to make a long story short again, I did not have the money to get the sound printed on the film, so I wanted to go back in time when films were silent and musicians would be performing as the films were being screened and take the jury on that trip with me. So I got dressed up and put on my white suit, which I used to wear for very special occasions. The musicians were dressed up too. We had a drum set, a clarinet and some other instruments. I was standing behind the wooden pedestal with the text I had written as the narration and a toy gun in the inner pocket of my jacket to make the one and only sound effect. I gave the jury members ties and 3D glasses to wear, out of the suitcase I was travelling back and forth between the continents. There were three professors on my board and senior students had asked for permission to participate in my moderation film screening. They were sitting close to the front, kind of in front of me and the jury members were sitting in the middle, a little bit to the back. It went great as expected.

The only technical problem was that the toy gun did not make a sound like a "BANG" at the scene where I had planned, but that was all right because I could see that we had achieved what I had planned in my mind which was to take them on a journey with me just like in the old times when films were silent and to blow their minds. I think I did it. The look in their eyes gave me that feeling. They had never seen anything as crazy and bold as that before in the movie theater probably, but they did not pass me. We had a board meeting with the professors right across from Prof. Adolfas Mekas' office upstairs and the sound room, which was full of big expensive machines and delicate electronic equipment. They told me that I hadn't passed. I was surprised because I thought that it had gone really well and the adrenaline was still in my veins as well as the looks in their eyes. I honestly thought that it was not fair to fail someone after such a challenging screening because all I could not do was a technical matter which solely depended on money, which I did not have, although I worked at the theater as a carpenter, painter and electrician as well as at the dishwashing room in the evenings at the dining hall. In other words, I had shown them that I could do everything that needed to be done for this soundtrack live as the film rolled and it was definitely much more harder than paying some technicians at some sound studio and lab to do it for you. I think Adolfas knew what I was talking about and although he did not directly literally support me right then at that point in time, but he did something very special and daring that meant to me a whole lot more and what he did right then stuck with me as one of my greatest memories at Bard. He went and got this poster that I had given him with a black and white picture of a man wearing a suit and a hat with his pants rolled up to his knees standing in the water. Maybe it was the sea or maybe the ocean but this picture reminded me of him and I had written seven questions about the necessity of cinema on the back of the poster. I had picked a rock like a small pebble and given the poster to him with the pebble and the note I had written to inspire him to throw at the water in the picture. So he went and got it and told me to hold it and he threw the rock at the water and through the poster in the room with all the equipment and the monitors in the back. He was laughing and having a blast while the other professors were frozen ice cold in shock. That was a very special and unique moment for me. We were not getting along very well until then but after that incident everything changed and we became friends. He truly had a great soul. I miss him.

The New York Times

Adolfas Mekas, 85, Avant-Garde Filmmaker and Teacher

By BRUCE WEBER

Adolfas Mekas, a Lithuanian immigrant who became an influential avant-garde filmmaker and teacher and who, with his brother Jonas, founded Film Culture, the seminal journal for cineastes, died on Tuesday in Poughkeepsie, N.Y. He was 85.

The cause was heart failure, his wife, Pola Chapelle, said.

Though Jonas Mekas, a prolific director and avant-garde film archivist, became the better-known sibling, Adolfas Mekas made a handful of films that endure as avant-garde landmarks. The best known of them, "Hallelujah the Hills," a comedy that spoofed movie history in telling an elliptical tale about two young men and their slapstick pursuit of the same girl, was among the critical and popular hits of the inaugural New York Film Festival in 1963.

"Hallelujah" was praised at the festival alongside films by Alain Resnais ("Muriel"), Roman Polanski ("Knife in the Water"), Luis Buñuel ("The Exterminating Angel") and Joseph Losey ("The Servant").

The New York Times called the film "a modest little Vermont-made farce" that "surprised and delighted" the audiences "by boisterously affirming that life can be a ball and movie-making can be fun."

Mr. Mekas (pronounced MEEK-us) and his brother arrived in New York in 1949, having survived a Nazi labor camp at the end of World War II. Sons of a farmer with a love of books and movies, they plunged into the bohemian intellectual life of the city in the early 1950s, founding Film Culture, a pioneering journal that began in 1955 with the then-presumptuous notion that movie-making was a serious art form and a potent influence on the culture at large.

With contributors including Andrew Sarris, Stan Brakhage, Richard Leacock, Rudolf Arnheim, Arlene Croce and Peter Bogdanovich, it championed the

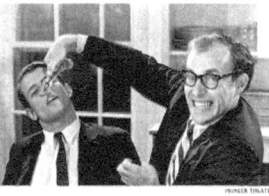 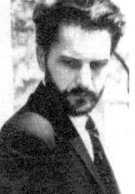

PIONEER THEATER

Above, Peter H. Beard, left, and Marty Greenbaum in "Hallelujah the Hills," by Adolfas Mekas. Right, Mr. Mekas in 1982.

MUSEUM OF THE MOVING IMAGE

avant-garde, though it gave thoughtful coverage to mainstream movie-making as well. (The journal ceased publication in the 1990s.)

Mr. Mekas, who lived in Rhinebeck, N.Y., was a founding member of the film department at Bard College in Annandale-on-Hudson, N.Y., and taught there from 1971 to 2004; he directed its film program from 1971-1994.

Adolfas Mekas was born in a Lithuanian village called Seme-

A Lithuanian immigrant and his brother, both obsessed with movies.

---

niskiai (pronounced sem-uh-NEESH-kee) on Sept. 30, 1925. During the final year of World War II, he and Jonas were leaving Lithuania to join an uncle in Austria when they were captured by the Germans and sent to a labor camp. After the war ended, they lived in refugee camps, one of which was in Mainz, near Frankfurt, where they were able to attend university classes. They first thought of leaving for Israel.

"They weren't Jewish," Ms. Chapelle said, "but they thought

it was romantic, to fight for a new country" — but emigrated instead to the United States, settling in Williamsburg, in Brooklyn.

"It was all just misery and dislocation and suffering and loss," Jonas Mekas wrote of their early years in Europe. But arriving in New York City changed their lives.

"Now, suddenly everything was bright, exciting and available," he wrote. "The streets of New York were open markets, like something out of Cairo. We bought three or four oranges on our first day. Here we are! We can buy fruit!"

In 1971, the Mekas brothers returned to Lithuania for the first time since their departure, and each made a film of the trip, Jonas's called "Reminiscences of a Journey to Lithuania," Adolfas's "Going Home." They were shown together at the New York Film Festival in 1972, an evening described by Vincent Canby in The Times as "rather more brimful of Mekases than one might ordinarily seek out, yet it's also successively moving, indulgent, beautiful, poetic, banal, repetitious and bravely, heedlessly, personal."

In addition to his brother, who still lives in Brooklyn, now in Greenpoint, and his wife, whom he met at a movie screening and married in 1966, Mr. Mekas is sur-

vived by another brother, Costas, of Semeniskiai, and a son, Sean, of Rhinebeck.

His other films include "The Brig" (1964), directed by both brothers, an adaptation of a grim play performed by the Group Theater about Marines confined in a military prison, and "Windflowers" (1968), an elegiac, Vietnam-era story of a draft dodger who is shot trying to escape from the F.B.I.

At his death, Mr. Mekas was working on a film about Giordano Bruno, an Italian thinker who was burned at the stake as a heretic in 1600. Mr. Mekas described Bruno as "the first beatnik" and called the film, with typical cheek, "Burn, Bruno, Burn."

His wife said she was initially drawn to him by his unexpected, demonstrative humor; on their first date, he threw his hat out the window of a taxi cab, she recalled. Another time, after a film opening at the Museum of Modern Art, he rolled up the red carpet, put it under his arm and walked away with it, as if to take it home. (No one stopped him, she said, but he brought it back.)

"These two guys," she said about the Mekas brothers. "I always told our son: They came to this country with $10. They couldn't speak the language, and they started the first serious film journal in English. Not bad."

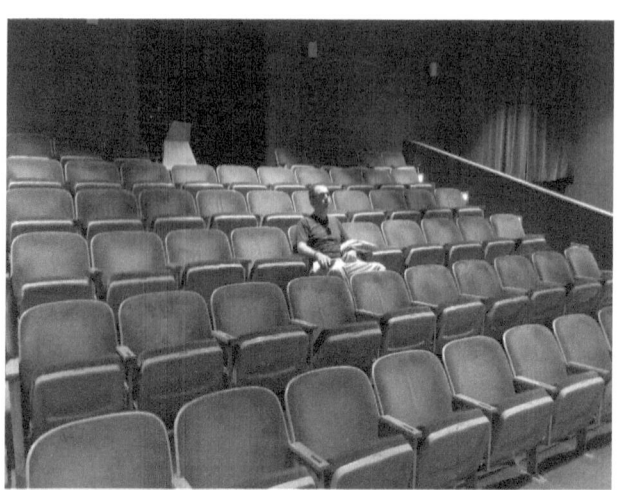

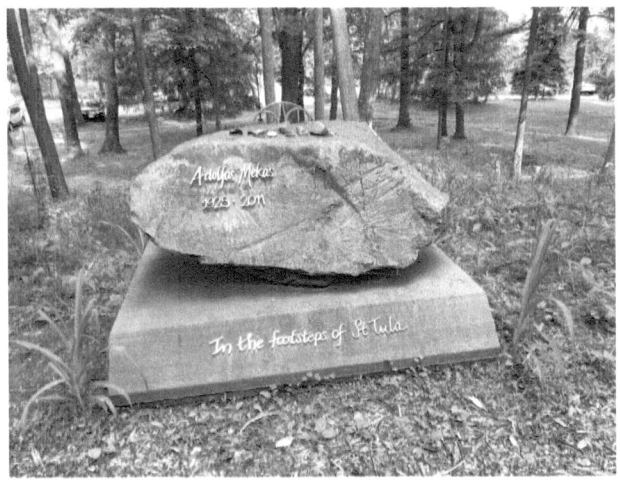

When I went to visit his grave I saw a huge rock as his gravestone with his name and it also said "In the footsteps of St. Tula" who represents the "spirit" of cinema. Some of his former students had left some small pebbles on his gravestone, which was that rock with the words, his name, and on the other side was the film reel stuck to the rock. May his soul rest in peace.

It is a very difficult concept to accept death. People live and die. But it is not and should not be that simple. Most other living things and animals live to survive and that is to eat, drink water, sleep and mate to reproduce their species. We are similar in that way but we are also capable of changing the way things are. The humans have transformed their own way of life so much in just a century. Technical inventions have been changing our daily life in a very drastic speed. The problem with this situation is the fact that humans are taking too many high risks, which are not in tune with nature, therefore causing the extinction of animals, plants and harming the natural cycle of life. We should evaluate and take into account all the long-term dangers that the scientific developments might cause. Now they are talking about massive changes that we might be witnessing even in our own life span such as choosing the specific characteristics of children before they are born or making eternal life possible. For example, parents will be able to decide about the color of their unborn children's hair or eyes. Humans are likely to be engineered and designed in the near future which is a scary and crazy idea.

In New York City we went to the same block that we used to live on and had a couple beers. I told my friend something; she took out her notebook to write it down. I guess it sounded too weird to be true but this is how it might be in the near future. "They will take your cells produce tissues and organs from them and then sell them back to you!" That is how it's going to be. They might be doing it even now. This is one of the reasons why I like science fiction. Yet we are in a phase in the history of civilization where we can not really distinguish between what is real and what is science fiction anymore. The reason why I chose to make a science-fiction film is also related to my interest in science, technology and ethics.

Now I would like to return back to the stories behind one of the scenes that we had a hard time shooting in New York. I wanted to shoot a scene in the rain but that made it particularly difficult because the equipment gets wet and they break down. So I spent a lot of my years getting excited when it started to rain. In a budgeted film production it is not such a big deal because you just call the company that makes it rain for you. They come to the location, set up pipes and hoses and make it look like it is raining but even in very high budget movies such as "Seven" (1995) by David Fincher, they couldn't get it quite right because the amount and intensity of the rain in one shot would not match the next. So in one scene the two main characters are sitting in a car and in each close up we see that the rain is not the same in the back. In one shot it is pouring on one side of the windshield and in the next it is just drizzling. I am not really so keen on such editing or production analysis yet I suppose it is a professional deformation, habit or defect. Anyway, since we did not have any company to make it look like it was raining, I had to wait for it to really rain and one time when I was living in Brooklyn it started to rain and I was hanging out with two Polish friends of mine at the time. So I told them about the scene and asked them if they would like to help me. They were hesitant in the beginning, because people do not want to go out in the rain in general, unless they are living in a country where it rains most of the time. Then, it is not a big deal because it becomes a common part of daily life so it is not such a special occasion. After a couple of drinks I convinced them to help me. They were kind enough to go out in the rain to this specific location around Morgan Avenue in Brooklyn, where there were empty industrial streets and avenues with warehouses and deserted areas and abandoned factories or buildings made out of bricks so it was a perfect setting for that scene in the film, which is in the beginning where the man who later turns out to be Seintn runs down the street trying to run away from himself or his invisible enemy. It was actually a dangerous neighborhood as well, so I must say that we were quite brave to be filming out there around that area in the middle of the night. Now I am sure it is much different and most likely gentrified. Back then I had lived close to that area with an ex-girlfriend of mine for a while, so I had an idea about the neighborhood and the kind of street I was looking for and it was right there. So I set up the camera while my friends held an umbrella over me. We didn't have much time and we were already getting wet so I set the aperture which was probably as wide as it could get on the 16mm lens and told my friends to press the button on my Bolex camera when I got out of the frame and ran to the other end of the street. I was wearing the brown jacket I used as a costume for the character of Seintn. By the way you might be wondering why the name of the character is Seintn. It is actually a combination of "Saint" and "Satan". I changed it around a little, not to make it too obvious and that is why I am writing this book to explain the intricate details behind the stories, characters and the scenes in the film. As a matter of fact, I would not be exaggerating if I told you that the background of the story in the film is much more detailed and thought out as the setting of the film. The film presents a part or a segment or a smaller fraction of the actual reality of the film, which I designed in my mind. There's a setting like a world where the stories in the film take place. I believe that is very important to do, so that you know what kind of a situation or technological environment and civilization you are placing your characters in. That way you have a better grasp and view of the reality you are trying to create in the film. Anyway, so I ran away to the other end of the street in the dark. There were just a few streetlights and the light was reflecting from the surface of the puddles and the wet pavement. We had only 30 seconds to shoot the scene and there was no time to rehearse because it was raining like cats and dogs and we were getting wet, hoping that the camera was okay. So the camera started rolling and I turned the corner running like a mad man in the rain. I stopped and turned around to see who was following me for a second and began to run again. We did two or three takes. I wouldn't be able to see how it turned out until it came back from the lab. But we were lucky. It turned out OK. The camera was still working fine and it hadn't gotten too wet, so I dried it and put it back in the camera bag. It is a wonderful yet strange feeling when you work with film because you don't know how it will look and you do some crazy things in front of the camera presuming that it will turn out fine, but you don't really know for sure until the rolls of film get back to you from the lab and all you can do is to do your best in front of the camera and behind it, setting it up, and later wait and hope that everything works out at the end.

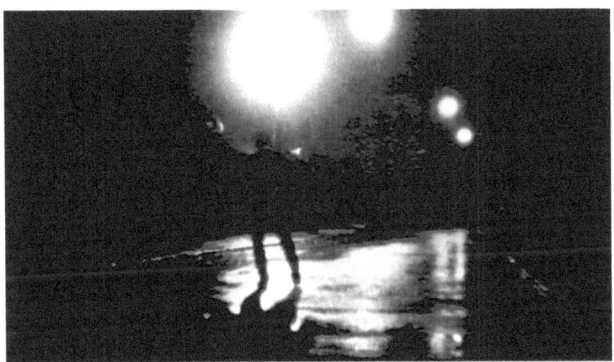

I am happy that I learned how to work with film as a materials and that the scene turned out alright. I used to work with this kind of cheaper lab down in Manhattan. It was called A-1. After I returned back to Turkey I mailed out a couple of rolls to get them developed there again, but unfortunately they got lost and I never got them back because the lab had closed. Many if not all labs went out of business around the world since they stopped producing film, which is kind of sad in my opinion because I worked with it so much and the intricate craftsmanship it required made you think and feel that you were working with a very exceptional and magical medium and art form. You do not quite get that when you are working with digital.

There is one very crucial fact that we have to be aware of while reading and analyzing these reminiscences and also other texts and memoirs which is that the technology available at the time when we were making the film was very limited. There were no waterproof cameras accessible such as GoPros. So we have to bear in mind that the circumstances were much different and definitely technologically less advanced back then. Yet easy things or less demanding tasks do not provide as big of a satisfaction as the great challenges. Speaking of difficult challenges I almost forgot to make a tribute to a few of the most rigorous scenes we had to overcome during the production of the film. One of these was the opera scene, which I ended up shooting in a couple of locations in different countries. Many thanks to Begüm

Mengü who is an amazing opera singer whose talent is beyond imagination. She helped me out with this scene by coming all the way from Ankara to Istanbul to sing for the film. She is a professional opera singer. I had been trying to tackle this scene for a pretty long time. She was a friend of my friends so we got in touch and she came to act and sing in the film. I am truly very grateful for that. We had been looking for a location to film at a grand stage and we searched all the theaters, opera houses and even old movie theaters and historical buildings. The famous Emek Building was about to be demolished with the magnificent historical cinema along with it. We tried to save the building by going to the protests and by trying to preserve it at least as an image on film yet it did not help unfortunately. We did all we could to get in touch with the owners but it was too late. There was nothing we could do to save the building or shoot the scene inside it. So I thought of other alternatives such as the historical opera house of Yıldız Palace, which was built during the Ottoman Empire. We applied for an permission to visit and evaluate the location and that process took quite some time to begin with. Once we got the permission we went to see the opera house but unfortunately there was a problem with the lighting due to a fire hazard since it is a very old wooden historical site they do not let any lights to be used in the building and the natural sunlight entering the building was not efficient enough to shoot a scene over there. So we kept looking.

After a few more attempts to find an appropriate opera house I decided to go for the stage that you see in the film which is not exactly an opera house but that one was the only one that looked like a classic old stage with the big golden colored frame made out of carved wood above the stage and with red velvet curtains. It was a cold winter day. My street was covered with ice and snow so it was impossible to get a cab because it was almost a state of emergency therefore there were not any taxies available at all so we had to walk up the hill with all the equipment, to a place we would maybe have a better chance. We had selected the costume for the scene and the part she was going to perform was also ready. The only problem was that we could not get there. Many people would have quit or postponed the shooting but we didn't and that is absolutely the virtue of Begüm because she did not give up under those very difficult circumstances and it did not have anything to do with money or anything because she was doing it voluntarily. And audio technician friend of mine also came with us to record the sound. Thanks to her as well. Everything went well after we got there. Actually I suppose getting there was the hardest part. Since she is a top-notch professional opera singer she knew the part by heart. We had discussed the way we were going to do it so we got it perfect after a few takes. Later some people might have thought that the scene resembles a little bit of a scene in "Mulholland Drive" (2001) by David Lynch but it doesn't have anything to do with it because it is not an opera performance in that film and the music keeps playing after the singer collapses on the stage but in our scene she falls at the stage and the opera piece stops because it is a real performance. The main differences are the facts that she is lip-synching in that movie but she is really singing in ours and it is a part in the opera piece where the performance is disrupted by the falling of the character in the opera "Tosca" by Puccini. So in other words the singing is fake in the other one. But briefly what is emphasized in my opera scene is the gap between reality and fantasy or the doubt about truth and illusion. She drops in the middle of the scene and the audience does not know if it is a serious "real" fall or if it is part of the performance. So it is about the suspense between the initial human reaction to the real case of urgency or death and the performed crisis on stage, which also addresses the conflict between the representation of reality in art and the actual reality that we accept as our every day life. Another interesting aspect of that scene, apart from the story of finding the location and the difficulty of getting there, was the preparations taking very long and the scene being rather short compared to the time we spent to make it happen. Also one more very fundamental difference between the two scenes is the meaning or the message they deliver. In Mulholland Drive the story is about a girl who wants to be an actress and eventually become famous. So the scene that seems to be similar represents the fakeness of the entertainment business especially in the US because the performance on stage is not "real". That is revealing that the show is a hoax, which is indicated by the singer not actually singing but pretending to be singing and the performers being like expendable and replaceable pawns in a bigger game. And the show goes on even if the singer, the performer, the actor or the actress falls or dies because it is an artificial system that works regardless of the pawns who are working for it. Yet, in our scene the idea is entirely different. It is more about the discussion that René Magritte raises with his painting titled "Treachery of Images" (1928) with the words "Ceci n'est pas une pipe." written under the painted image of a pipe and the argument that Michel Foucault brings up in his book based on or referring to that specific painting.

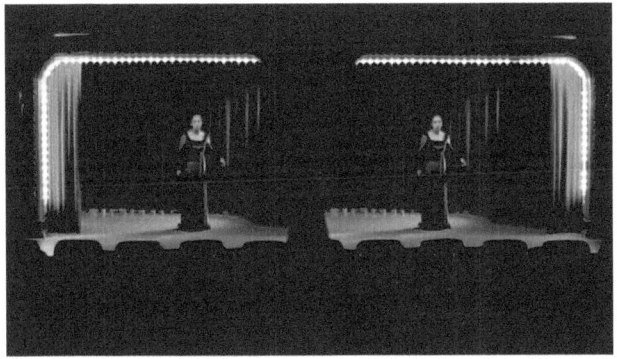

Returning back to the stories behind the opera scene I shot the establishing shot of the sequence in Paris when I was visiting the city for one of my film screenings. I was invited by an organization that was putting together a festival / exhibition and a series of conferences, which were taking place in a few major cities in Europe. So I got permission from the university I was teaching at, to leave and attend these activities and applied for a visa to go to Paris. I was going to stay at a friend's apartment there. She helped me out a lot as well. Thanks to Didem Yalınay and Görkem Ünal as well as Deniz and Ela Altay for all their support. I asked Didem (my actress friend) if she would like to come to Paris with me to act in the opera scene after seeing that the screening of my film was going to be at a historical theater. So I figured we could take this opportunity to film in the building since we were going to be invited to attend the screening. That plan did not work out unfortunately. I don't quite remember exactly what it was about but I remember going to the place and them telling us either that the screenings were rescheduled and that we had missed it or that we needed to apply for an official permit to film in the building which would take a very long time to get and we didn't have that much time since our visas were going to expire soon and I had my job at the university that I had to return to. I was pissed off because I had meticulously arranged everything to go there attend the screening, activities and to film the opera scene. Our first attempt was a failure. My initial plan had not worked out but I was not going to give up. So I came up with another idea. We went around town looking for a stainless steel platter with a cover but all we could get was a silver butter dish with a lid. We needed that for the opera glasses, which look like little binoculars that are served or made available at the opera houses. And some people bring their own I suppose. Anyway so I bought tickets for a play at an old theater building. We were going to get in costume, go to the theater and watch the play and during the intermission we would shoot the scene of the audience mise en scène of the opera sequence. It was a play by Shakespeare. We went there, found our seats, which were on the third or the fourth floor. I had the camera beside me in a bag. The act was quite long, I must say and there was a guy sitting in front of us who was laughing his ass off. He was pretty loud too. After a while it was intermission. It was our turn to shoot the scene and we didn't have much time to do it. We did not have any time to rehearse but we ended up having to do a couple of takes. I got what I needed finally and right then a security guard or a member of the staff came to tell me that it was not allowed to film in the theater but they were too late, we already had what we wanted so I put the camera away into the camera bag and we left. It was great. My first plan had failed but I came up with another plan, which is in a way like improvising which is essential when you are working like this without a budget, without permissions or anything and we did it. I would not recommend it but it is definitely more challenging and fun. I also went to the huge opera house that was located in a gigantic building in the middle of the city. It is The National Academy of Music.

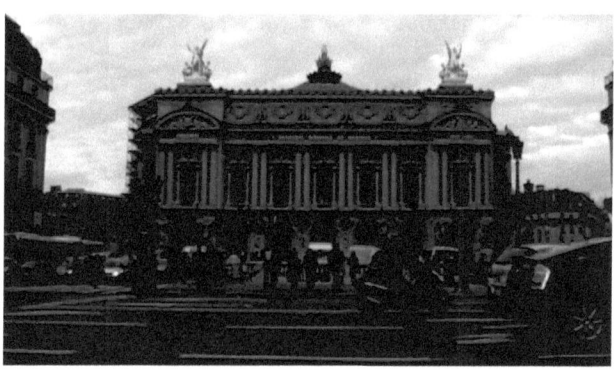

While I was shooting the establishing shot from a distance with my Bolex camera, an old lady spoke to me in French. She was I think happy to see that Bolex cameras were still being used. Well, they are not being used by everybody in general and I don't know if they even teach how to use a Bolex to film students anymore, but I think they are wonderful and I believe we were in agreement with that lady about that. Anyway I got into the building and started walking around with a tour yet later, I snuck into a balcony box where there were others watching the rehearsal. I took out my camera and started to get some shots of the space and the stage. It had an amazing ambience.

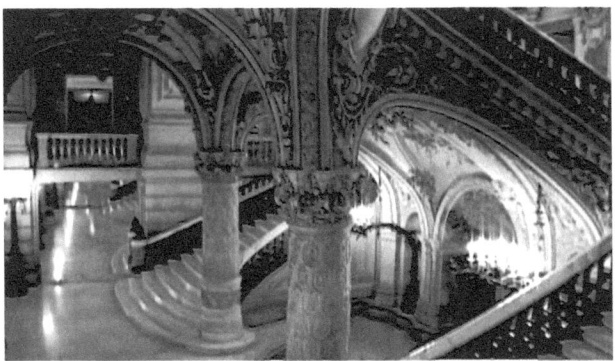

After a while I was the only one left. Someone from the security staff came and asked me if I work there and I shook my head trying not to shake the camera and the guy just left and l continued to film some more but I did not use much of that footage except for the little bits of the shots of the audience and the empty architectural spaces in the historic building. On my way out a black French security officer stopped me and asked me where I had been and what I had been doing since the tour had ended along time ago. I told him that I had a stomachache and that I had to leave the tour to go to the restroom. I don't know if he bought it but he let me go so I was feeling pretty content as I was walking out of the building. I shot some of the other scenes in different locations. I filmed the other two characters getting their opera glasses in two separate places but they all look like they are one place because of the way I edited them together. That is the magic of cinema. I actually intended to also make sure that the sequence was structured in such a way that it could be interpreted as the reflections of the same personality of the girl projected into variations or versions of reality.

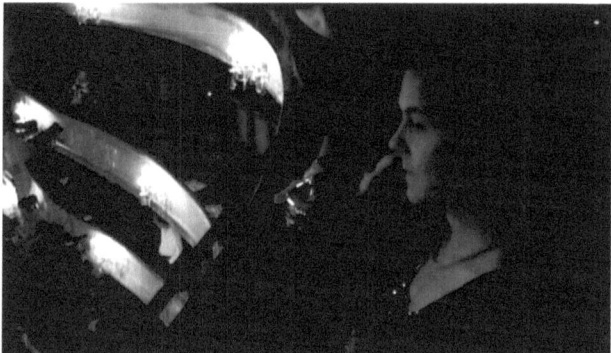

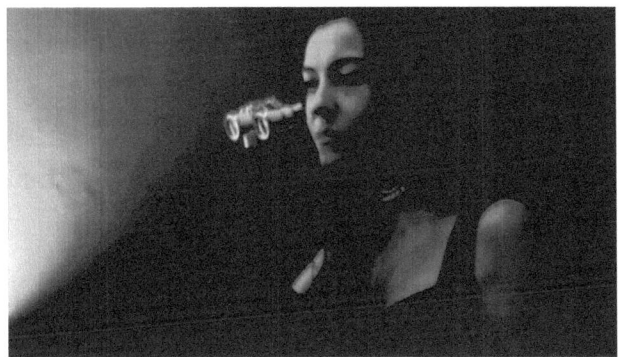

One of the strongest aspects of cinema is the editing. Because that is where the meaning is created. As the two or more images, visuals or sounds are juxtaposed something incredible happens and the dialectic function of cinematic elements begin to speak in their unique language. Some of the cuts are very fast therefore they are harder to notice. For instance the shot of Seintn throwing the empty bottle at the wall and smashing it to pieces was one of the difficult scenes because it was not easy to find a brick wall that we could break a bottle on without getting into trouble. A friend of mine who is an architect told me that she was renovating a place where there was an old brick wall so we went there and shot that scene with some lights to illuminate the place because we needed a lot of light to get it on film. It would have been totally unnoticeable if we hadn't shot it a bit slower such as at 32 frames per second instead of 24 as in slow motion and that requires more light. It is such short shot in the editing that you do not even get to really see it. There are quite a lot of different editing techniques that I employed in the film.

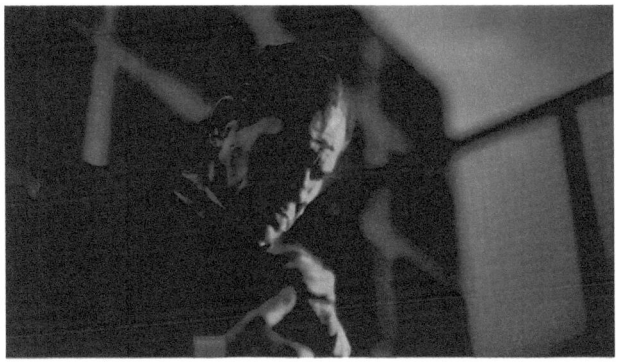

One of them is the editing in the scene where The White Man struggles to get out of the screen, which is a metaphorical juxtaposition of several shots of him scratching the surface of a transparent wall while particles are falling. That is a multi-layered editing method I used to reflect the psychological subconscious or dream state that the character is in. The commercial in the beginning of the film is edited with very quick cuts, which consist of two or three frames each.

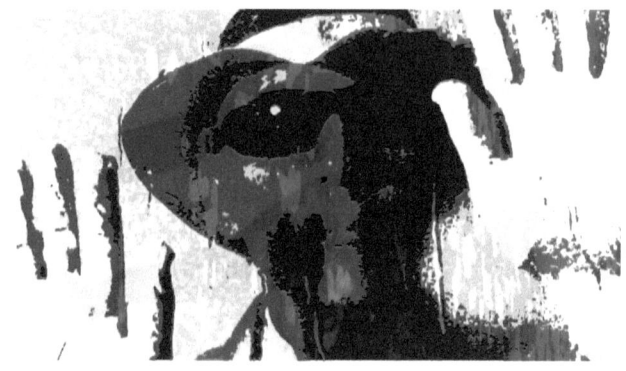

The rotating scene of the black and white room was shot in a big art center. I painted some black and white boards as the tiles for the floor. I had collected a sink and a toilet bowl and I brought a chair that would fit the set-up of the room in the scene. We couldn't shoot just anywhere because it had to be a bird's eye view so the perspective of the cinematography required the camera to be high up and we did not have a drone because it was not invented back then or a crane, which is the enormous mechanical device, or equipment which they use for such angles in the industry. So I figured that I could shoot from the top floor of the art exhibition space where we were having an art exhibition at the time. I just had a 16mm and a 25mm lens so I had to be high up enough to fit everything in the frame. I laid down the tiles and the props and that is how I prepared the set-up or the stage for that scene.

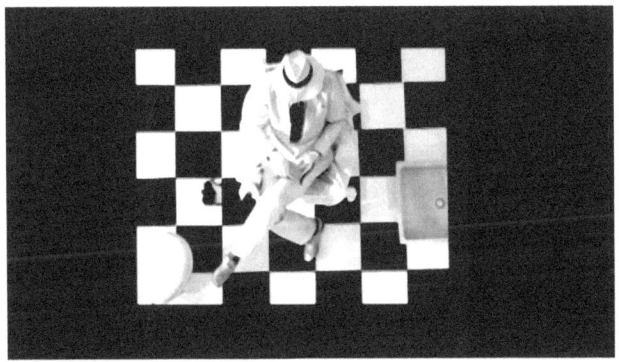

I do not want to write a conclusion or give advice about anything but all I would like to say to the people who are eager to do something such as making a film under very tough circumstances or against impossibilities is that they should try to achieve their goals no matter what and they should try not to go for the common, standard or regular solutions but they should try to invent and create their own way of doing things. I might as well add that if it does not work out at the end, I guess we should not push it too hard either. Good luck to all who have crazy dreams. Don't forget to make your wishes to the Goddess of Cinema, St. Tula. That is one thing I forgot to do and maybe that is why it took me so long to finish the film.

One or two other things I forgot to write about are the desert and the bird scenes. We shot a part of the desert at White Sands, which is a place in New Mexico where it is a rumor that they tested the atom bomb for the first time and because of that it is said that the sand turned into glass due to the extreme heat wave that was emitted. A large section of the desert is not open to public since there is probably still radioactive residue. The other part where we see the man (acted by me) with a white suit, a white hat, a white umbrella and a white suitcase walking on the dune of sand was shot at Patara, in Turkey. It was

very hot and I had to convince my friends and my
brother to help me shoot the scene when we were on a
road trip. I had to carry all the costumes with me so that I
would be able to film the scenes when I was at a suitable
location to shoot at. The make-up was so thick that it
took a couple of days for it to completely disappear from
my face.

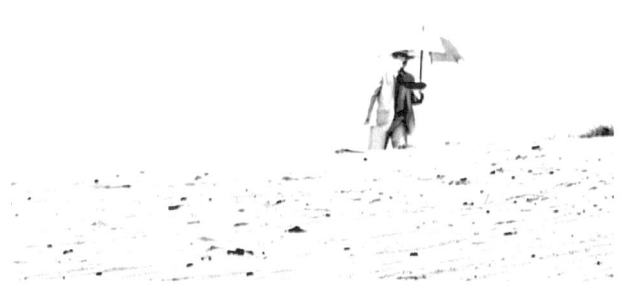

And maybe most importantly the birds that came to help with the filming were the most magical components of the production. All the birds in the film are real; they are not created with visual or special effects in the post-production. They came and participated in the making of the film and they did it magnificently as they always do. Thanks to those wonderful birds and all the people who helped out with the making of this particular film.

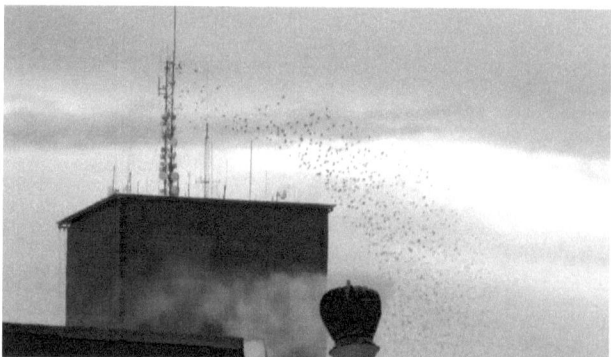